WITHD

This book to be returned on or before

| 5 JAN 2000 | | |
| 2 6 JAN 2000 | | |

346.41 072

Willett, C. G.

Sale and supply of goods: quality obligations and remedies

CCTA LIBRARIES LLYRGELLAU CCTA

SALE AND SUPPLY OF GOODS

Quality Obligations
and
Remedies

SALE AND SUPPLY OF GOODS

Quality Obligations
and
Remedies

by
Christopher Willett
Aidan ODonnell

CLT PROFESSIONAL PUBLISHING
A DIVISION OF CENTRAL LAW TRAINING LTD

© Christopher Willett, Aidan ODonnell 1996

Published by:
CLT Professional Publishing
A Division of Central Law Training Ltd
Wrens Court
52-54 Victoria Road
Sutton Coldfield
Birmingham B72 1SX

ISBN 1 85811 068 8

All rights reserved. No part of this publication may be reproduced, stored in a retrieval system, or transmitted in any form or by any means, electronic, mechanical, photocopying, recording or otherwise, without the prior written permission of the publisher.

The moral right of the authors has been asserted.

CCTA LIBRARIES LLYRGELLAU CCTA	
Morley Books	25.8.99
346.41	£16.00
R029357	

Typeset by Cheryl Zimmerman
Printed in Great Britain by The Lavenham Press Ltd

Contents

Preface	vii
Table of Statutes	viii
Table of Cases	ix
Introduction	**1**
1. Exemption Clauses	**7**
2. The Quality Obligation	**19**
3. Remedies	**33**
Appendix I: Relevant Provisions of the Unfair Contract Terms Act 1977	47
Appendix II: Previous Legislative Provisions: Sale of Goods Act 1979, Sections 11, 14, 15, 30, 34, 35	51
Appendix III: Text of the Sale and Supply of Goods Act 1994	55
Appendix IV: Amended Legislative Provisions: Sale of Goods Act 1979, Sections 14, 15, 15A, 30, 34, 35, 35A	81
Appendix V: Specimen Contract for Sale	87
Appendix VI: Specimen Contract for the Hire of Goods	91
Appendix VII: Specimen Hire-Purchase Agreement	95
Index	99

Preface

This book aims to review the main rules on the quality obligation in contracts for sale and supply of goods, and remedies for breach of the quality obligation.

It seeks, where possible, to integrate practical advice as to drafting terms and conditions in the light of the rules. There are, of course, a wealth of excellent commercial law sources which must be turned to for detailed analysis of certain issues *e.g.* Goode on *Commercial Law*, Bradgate and Savage on *Commercial Law*, And Bradgate on *Standard Terms of Trading*.

This book was primarily written to provide a practical guide to the new provisions and to provide access to these provisions. We have, among other things, used the Appendices to set out the 1994 Act, and separately, to set out the provisions in their amended form.

Christopher Willett
Aidan ODonnell
June 1996

Table of Statutes

Sale of Goods Act 1979
s 1 3
s 6(4) 29
s 11 34
s 11(3) 2
s 11(4) 2, 5, 41
s 13 1
s 14 ....1, 3, 5, 20, 22, 23, 27
s 14(1) 22, 29
s 14(2) 22, 24, 26, 29
s 14(5) 27, 28, 29
s 15 ....1, 20
s 15A 3, 5, 35, 43
s 15B 3, 5, 34, 43
s 20 29
s 27 ....42, 43
s 30(4) 2
s 35 ....3, 5, 36, 37
s 35(1) 41
s 35(2) 38, 39
s 35(5) 39, 40
s 35A 3, 5, 41
s 53(1) 44, 45
s 53(2) 43
s 53(3) 43, 44

Sale & Supply of Goods Act 1994
s 1 ....3, 20
s 2 ....36, 41
s 3 ....3, 41
s 4 ....3, 34

Sale & Supply of Goods Act 1994
— *cont.*
s 5 ....3, 34
s 7 ....1, 3
Sched 2 ....1, 3

Unfair Contract Terms Act 1977
s 1(3) 29
s 2 9
s 3(2)(b) 35, 36
s 5 9
s 6 ....8, 11, 25, 27, 40, 45
s 6(4) 29
s 7 ....8, 9, 10, 11, 25, 27, 40, 45
s 11 ....8, 13, 25, 27, 40, 45
s 11(1) 11
s 11(2) 11
s 11(4) 11, 12, 16, 25
s 11(5) 12
s 12 ....8, 10, 25
s 13 ....8, 9, 10, 40, 45
s 17(1)(b) 36
s 20 ....8, 11, 25, 27, 29
s 21 ....8, 11, 25, 27
s 21(3) 29
s 24 ....8, 11, 25, 27, 45
s 24(3) 11
s 25 ....8, 25, 45
s 25(1) 10
Sched 2 ....8, 12, 13, 45
Sched 2(b) 14, 25
Sched 2(c) 14, 25

Table of Cases

Aswan Engineering Establishment v Lupdine [1987] 1 WLR 1 ....24, 31

Bernstein v Pamson Motors, [1987] 2 All ER 220CA 39, 40, 46
Boyter v Thomson [1995] 3 All ER 135 ....28, 31
Buchanan-Jardine v Hamilink and Another 1983 SLT 149....................22, 31

Davies v Sumner [1984] 1 WLR 1301 ....21, 31

Farnworth Finance v Attryde [1970] 2 All ER 774 ....37, 46
Fred Chappell Ltd v NCP Ltd, *The Times*, 9 May 1978 ....15, 17

George Mitchell v Finney Lock Seeds [1983] 2 AC 803..14, 16, 17, 25, 44, 45
GKN Centrax Gears Ltd v Matbro Ltd [1976] 2 Lloyd's Rep 555, CA.....44, 46
Godley v Perry [1960] 1 WLR 9..44
Green, RW, Ltd v Cade Bros Farms [1978] 1 Lloyd's Rep 602 ....14, 17, 25

Hadley v Baxendale (1854) 9 Exch 341 ....43, 46
Hyslop v Shirlaw (1905) 7F 875 ....40, 46

Johnstone v Bloomsbury Health Authority [1991] 2 All ER 293 ....9, 17

Knight Machinery v Rennie 1995 SLT 166 ....14, 17, 25

Lambert v Lewis [1982] AC 225 ....26, 31

Millar's of Falkirk v Turpie 1976 SLT 66..25, 31

Phillips Products v Hyland [1987] 2 All ER 620................................16, 17, 25

R and B Customs Brokers Co Ltd v United Dominions Trust Ltd
[1988] 1 All ER 847 ....10, 17, 21, 31
Rogers v Parish (Scarborough) Ltd [1987] 2 All ER 232........................25, 31

Schroeder Music Publishing Co Ltd v Macaulay [1974] 3 All ER 616.....14, 17
Smith v Bush; Harris v Wyre Forest DC [1989] 2 All ER 514, HL........9, 13, 17

ix

Smith v Wheatsheaf Mills Ltd [1939] 2 KB 302 ....42, 46
Stewart Gill Ltd v Horatio Myer and Co Ltd [1992] 2 All ER 257 9

Waldron Kelly v BRB [1981] 3 Cur Law 33...15, 17
Woodman v Photo Trade Processing (1981) 131 NLJ 935 ....16, 17, 25, 46

Introduction

This book deals with the quality obligation which arises by statutory implication in contracts for the sale, hire-purchase, hire and transfer of property in goods; the remedies for breach of this obligation; and the extent to which the obligation itself and/or the remedies may be excluded or limited by express contractual terms. Our aim is to give practitioners, academics and students a clear account of the rules in question, and to consider the contracting options which the rules in question give to the parties. It is fundamental to our approach that the discussion should be relevant to practitioners, and so the legal implications of using particular types of terms and clauses are discussed. The book is designed to be accessible to busy practitioners, and includes relevant advice throughout the text along with summary charts at the end of chapters and source materials in the appendices.

The issue of quality obligations and remedies is particularly topical at present as the Sale and Supply of Goods Act 1994 has significantly amended the rules contained in the existing legislation.

History

Since the last century there has been a statutorily recognised term imposing an obligation of quality upon those selling goods in the course of a business. This has existed as part of a package of implied terms, the others relating to description, compliance with sample, and fitness for purpose. Originally these terms only had a statutory basis in the case of contracts for the sale of goods (see Sale of Goods Act 1979, ss 13-15). However, the implied terms were extended to contracts of hire-purchase by the Supply of Goods (Implied Terms) Act 1973. They were later extended to contracts of hire and contracts for the transfer of property in goods by the Supply of Goods and Services Act 1982. However, this Act only applied to England and Wales. In Scotland, the common law remained the source of implied obligations on these matters. However, the Sale and Supply of Goods Act 1994 (s 7 and Sched 2) has extended the provisions of the Supply of Goods Services Act to Scotland (see below at pp 61-69).

SALE AND SUPPLY OF GOODS

Difficult issues

There are a number of issues in relation to the quality obligation and the remedies attached to it, which have always been difficult and have been subject to considerable political and academic discussion over the years.

First of all there has always been difficulty with the quality standard itself. How many purposes did a product need to be fit for? Did it need to be durable? To what extent (if at all) was quality to be determined by aesthetic criteria?

Then there is the question of remedies. Where there is a breach of the quality obligation damages are always available. There is also a rejection remedy. The key difficulty here is that in sales contracts this remedy is lost when goods have seen "accepted", the question being what exactly amounted to "acceptance". For example, did it amount to acceptance to agree to a repair, to effect a sub-sale or to sign an acceptance note?

Another difficulty (for buyers in particular) arose from the fact that where part of a batch of goods was qualitatively defective the buyer under a contract of sale could only reject these (subject to the acceptance rules) if he rejected the whole batch. Acceptance of part of the batch amounted to acceptance of the whole batch (Sale of Goods Act 1979, ss 11(4), 30(4)).

Another problem was that in sales contracts (subject to the acceptance rules) the rejection remedy was always available no matter how minor the breach of the primary obligation. This was clear from the classification of the obligation as a condition and from the fact that section 11(3) of the Sale of Goods Act seemed to indicate that breach of a condition always gave a right to reject. Although this might be said to foster certainty (especially important for the private consumer who may find it difficult enough to obtain redress), there is also an argument that scope existed for bad faith rejection by the buyer where the breach is small and the buyer simply wishes to escape from a bad bargain.

In other supply contracts the obligation was also a condition but it was less clear as to whether this gave an automatic right to reject for breach. As has been said, section 11(3) of the Sale of Goods Act seemed to indicate that breach of a condition always meant a right to reject (subject to the acceptance rules). However, such elaboration did not exist in the other statures, so it was unclear whether the courts were free to take a common law approach and focus more on the seriousness of the breach.

INTRODUCTION

The reforms

All of the above areas have been reformed by the 1994 Sale and Supply of Goods Act.

Section 1 of the 1994 Act amends section 14 of the Sale of Goods Act 1979, introducing a new **"satisfactory quality"** standard applicable to both consumer and commercial transactions of sale. The standard for hire purchase, hire and transfer of goods is the same (see 1994 Act, s 7, Sched 2, pp 69-79 below).

Section 2 reforms the rules on when the **right to reject** is lost by "acceptance" in contracts of sale. It amends section 35 of the Sale of Goods Act, placing more emphasis on the buyer's opportunity to examine the goods to check for conformity. Other contracts for the supply of goods continue to be covered by common law rules, where there is no concept of acceptance. The basic question is whether the buyer has 'affirmed' the contract, which he cannot do without knowledge of the defect.

Section 3 inserts a new section 35A into the Sale of Goods Act, which has the effect of allowing **partial rejection and partial acceptance** of a batch of goods in circumstances where some of the batch is defective. In other contracts for the supply of goods the rules on partial rejection are governed by common law rules.

Sections 4 and 5 add sections 15A and B respectively to the SGA. Section 15A has the effect of restricting a **commercial buyer's right to reject** where the breach is so slight as to make rejection unreasonable (applicable to England). Section 15B has the effect of restricting a commercial buyer's right to reject where the breach is not material (applicable to Scotland). The same approach is applied to other supply contracts by Schedules 1 and 2 to the 1994 Act.

Structure of this book

Chapter 1 gives an overview of the rules on exemption clauses which are relevant to the quality obligation and liability for breach of it.

Chapter 2 considers the quality obligation, its content, and when it applies.

Chapter 3 considers the rules on remedies.

SALE AND SUPPLY OF GOODS

There are seven appendices. The first sets out the provisions of the Unfair Contract Terms Act (UCTA) 1977 which are relevant to the quality obligation and remedies for its breach. The second appendix sets out the sale and supply rules on quality and remedies as they were before they were amended. The third provides the text of the Sale and Supply Goods Act 1994, and the fourth sets out the resulting amended provisions of the Sale of Goods Act 1979.

The fifth, sixth and seventh appendices contain sample contracts of sale, hire, and hire-purchase respectively.

A footnote on approach

For ease of approach the bulk of the discussion in the text is of the relevant provisions of the Sale of Goods Act 1979. References are made to equivalent or different rules applying to other contracts for the supply of goods.

INTRODUCTION

Summary chart of amendments introduced by the 1994 Sale and Supply of Goods Act to the Sale of Goods Act 1979

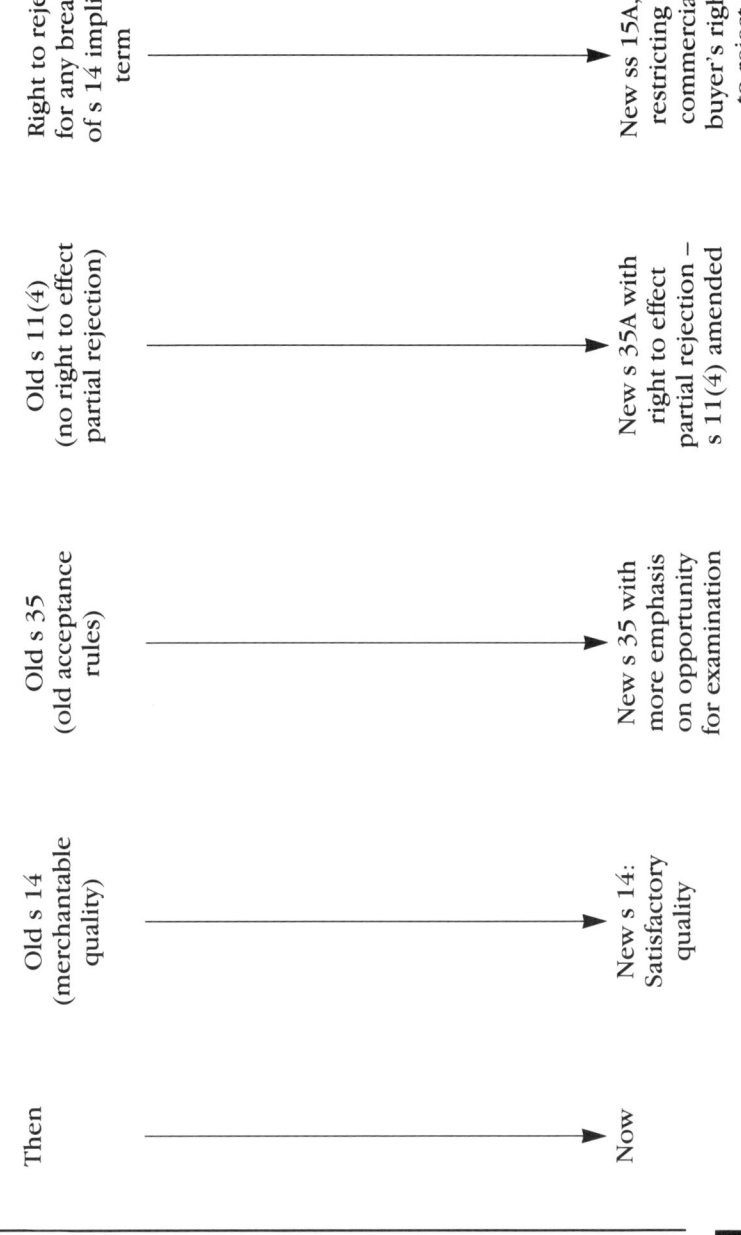

Then:
- Old s 14 (merchantable quality)
- Old s 35 (old acceptance rules)
- Old s 11(4) (no right to effect partial rejection)
- Right to reject for any breach of s 14 implied term

Now:
- New s 14: Satisfactory quality
- New s 35 with more emphasis on opportunity for examination
- New s 35A with right to effect partial rejection – s 11(4) amended
- New ss 15A, B restricting a commercial buyer's right to reject

CHAPTER 1
Exemption Clauses

Definition of an exemption clause under UCTA	8
Excluding or restricting liability	8
Who is a consumer?	10
Contracts not made "in the course of a business"	10
Holding oneself out as being in business	10
Goods "ordinarily supplied for private use or consumption"	11
Exemption in commercial sales	11
The reasonableness test	11
Limitation clauses	11
Schedule 2 criteria	12
Burden of proof on supplier	12
Summary of reasonableness so far	12
Key decisions	13
Bargaining power	13
Available alternatives	14
Difficulty of the task	15
Practical consequences	16
Key cases	17

SALE AND SUPPLY OF GOODS

CHAPTER I

Exemption Clauses

The chapters below discuss the quality obligation and the issues of rejection of goods which have been the subject of reform. However, these cannot be discussed fully without also considering the use of exemption clauses. The approach taken by most other books is to discuss exemption clauses *after* discussion of primary obligations and remedies. However we wished to analyse the obligations and remedies in the context of exemption clauses. In order to do this it is necessary to first set out the rules on exemption clauses contained in the Unfair Contract Terms Act (UCTA) 1977.

The relevant English sections of UCTA are sections 6, 7, 11, 12 and 13 and Schedule 2, which are reproduced below in Appendix I (the very similar Scottish provisions are contained in sections 20, 21, 24 and 25). The impact of these provisions is that the basic quality obligation and the remedies flowing from it cannot be excluded or restricted in consumer sales, and can only be excluded or restricted in non-consumer sales if the seller can prove the clause to be reasonable. First, however, we must consider what counts as an exemption clause under UCTA.

Definition of an exemption clause under UCTA

The definition of a clause excluding or limiting liability under UCTA is contained in section 13 (the Scottish equivalent is s 25). Section 13 clearly covers clauses which openly seek to exclude or limit liability for breach of the obligation in question. Section 13 also covers at least some types of clauses which in effect and substance, if not in form, attempt to reduce or extinguish the liability which would otherwise arise—for example by saying that there is no obligation in the first place.

Excluding or restricting liability

Section 13 of UCTA says that:

"(1) To the extent that this part of this Act prevents the exclusion or restriction of any liability it also prevents –

EXEMPTION CLAUSES

(a) making the liability or its enforcement subject to restrictive or onerous conditions" (*e.g. requiring the deposit of money with the supplier before a claim may be brought or requiring that claims be made within an unreasonably short period of time*);

"(b) excluding or restricting any right or remedy in respect of the liability, or subjecting a person to any prejudice in consequence of his pursuing any such might or remedy" (*e.g. restricting or excluding a customer's right to 'set off' their obligation to pay against the supplier's breach,[1] excluding or limiting a right to reject for breach of contract, or threatening to withhold further orders if the consumer takes action*);

(c) "excluding or restricting rules of evidence or procedure" (*e.g. claiming that the supplier's judgment on matters of breach of contract is final*);

"and (to that extent) sections 2 and 5 to 7 also prevent excluding or restricting liability by reference to terms and notices which exclude or restrict the relevant obligation or duty".

What does this last paragraph of section 13 mean for exemption clauses and the quality obligation? In one case the House of Lords had to deal with the application of this paragraph to an attempt to exclude a common law duty of care by the use of a notice. It was said that:

'the existence of the common law duty of care ... is to be judged by considering whether it would exist but for the notice ...' (*Smith* v *Bush* [1989] 2 All ER 514, per Lord Griffiths at 530).

So in deciding whether an obligation or duty exists, the notice is ignored.

It seems that a similar test is regarded as correct in the context of contractual duties to take care, (*Johnstone* v *Bloomsbury Health Authority* [1991] 2 ALL ER 293, and see Macdonald, "Mapping the Unfair Contract Terms Act 1977", (1994) JBL 441 at 444-47) and presumably by analogy, where the implied terms as to quality, fitness, description etc are concerned. This means that in deciding whether the satisfactory quality obligation exists, any exclusion or limitation clause is ignored. If the satisfactory quality obligation does exist then any clause which seeks to dilute it in the same way (*e.g.* by saying that goods need only be safe, but not satisfactory in other respects) will be subject to the UCTA controls as a term seeking to exclude or limit liability.

[1]*Stewart Gill Ltd* v *Horatio Myer and Co Ltd* [1992] 2 ALL ER 257.

SALE AND SUPPLY OF GOODS

Who is a consumer?

As we have said above there can be no exemption of liability (within the meaning of s 13) where the buyer is dealing as a consumer. But who deals as a consumer?

"Dealing as a consumer" is defined in section 12 (for the virtually identical Scottish provision see s25 (1)).

Section 12 says that a party is a consumer if:

"(1) (a) he neither makes the contract in the course of a business nor holds himself out as doing so; and

(b) the other party does make the contract in the course of a business; and

(c) in the case of a contract governed by the law of sale of goods or hire-purchase, or by section 7 of this Act, the goods passing under or in pursuance of the contract of a type ordinarily supplied for private use or consumption.

(2) But on a sale by auction or by competitive tender the buyer is not in any circumstances to be regarded as dealing as consumer.

(3) Subject to this, it is for those claiming that a party does not deal as consumer to show that he does not."

Contracts not made "in the course of a business"
The typical private buyer buying, for example, household goods, a vehicle, a holiday or insurance is not making the contract in the course of a business.

However, it has also been held that a business does not buy "in the course of a business" if the purchase is not an integral part of the business. A purchase will be integral if it is a one-off trade venture or it forms part of a frequent pattern of such purchases (*R and B Customs Brokers Co Ltd* v *United Dominions Trust Ltd* [1988] 1 All ER 847). This seems to mean that the average business is a consumer when it buys outside its own field, for example when an accountant buys an office carpet or a computer or a car (unless he does this regularly).

Holding oneself out as being in business
Even if someone would otherwise qualify as a consumer, the protection will be lost if that person has held himself out as buying in the course of a business—for example by the use of a trade card to obtain a discount.

EXEMPTION CLAUSES

Goods "ordinarily supplied for private use or consumption"
Goods must be of the type "ordinarily supplied for private use or consumption. Many forms of purchase will be entirely unproblematic. Cars, televisions, videos, washing machines, fridges etc are usually bought for private use (even if they are also sometimes bought for business use). It must also be the case that many types of computer equipment are ordinarily bought for private use. However, it would seem that an item such as an office chair, if purchased by a private consumer, would not be regarded as something "ordinarily supplied for private use or consumption".

Exemption in commercial sales
The seller can exempt liability where the buyer is not a consumer if he can show the exemption to be reasonable (ss 6, 7, 20 & 21). The reasonableness test is discussed below.

The reasonableness test

The basic test is contained in section 11(1) (see s 24 for Scotland)

> "In relation to a contract term, the requirement of reasonableness ... is that the term shall have been a fair and reasonable one to be included having regard to the circumstances which were, or ought reasonably to have been in the contemplation of the parties when the contract was made."

Clauses which limit (as opposed to exclude) liability are also subject to section 11(4).

Limitation clauses

> "Where by reference to a contact term or notice a person seeks to restrict liability to a specified sum of money, and the question arises (under this or any other Act) whether the term or notice satisfies the requirement of reasonableness, regard shall be had in particular ... to –
>
> (a) the resources which he could expect to be available to him for the purpose of meeting the liability should it arise; and
>
> (b) how far it was open to him to cover himself by insurance" (see s 24(3) for Scotland). [see further at p 16 below]

SALE AND SUPPLY OF GOODS

Schedule 2 Criteria

In cases where sellers attempt to exclude or restrict liability for breach of the implied terms as to description, quality and fitness in contracts for the sale and supply of goods, and the buyer is not a consumer, section 11(2) says that in application of the reasonableness test particular regard should be paid to the guidelines contained in Schedule 2 of the Act. These are:

> "(a) the strength of the bargaining positions of the parties relative to each other, taking into account (among other things) alternative means by which the customer's requirements could have been met;
>
> (b) whether the customer received an inducement to agree to the term, or in accepting it had an opportunity of entering into a similar contract with other persons but without having to accept a similar term;
>
> (c) whether the customer knew or ought reasonably to have known of the existence and extent of the term (having regard, among other things, to any custom of the trade and any previous course of dealing between the parties).
>
> (d) where the term excludes or restricts any relevant liability if some condition is not complied with, whether it was reasonable at the time of the contract to expect that compliance with that condition would be practicable;
>
> (e) whether the goods were manufactured processed or adapted to the special order of the customer."

Burden of proof on supplier

Section 11(5) places the burden of proof in relation to reasonableness on the party relying on the clause (*i.e.* the seller or supplier):

> "It is for those claiming that a contract term or notice satisfies the requirement of reasonableness to show that it does."

Summary of reasonableness so far

Where the courts are considering a clause excluding or limiting liability in the context of the quality obligation they must consider the Schedule 2 criteria, and where a limitation clause is concerned, the section 11(4) criteria. However the courts may look at other criteria as well. In order to see what these are we must look at a selection of cases. Many of these decisions are concerned with exemption of liability other than that for

EXEMPTION CLAUSES

breach of the quality obligation. However the criteria applied are still of relevance to exemption for breach of the quality obligation.

Key decisions

The only House of Lords judgment dealing squarely with the section 11 reasonableness test is the combined hearing of *Smith* v *Bush* and *Harris* v *Wyre Forest DC* [1989] 2 All ER 514. Having ruled that on the facts of both cases there was a duty of care in respect of a valuation carried out on behalf of a building society but passed to prospective purchasers (*i.e.* a duty of care to these purchasers), the House of Lords had to decide upon the reasonableness of relying on a term used to exclude liability for breach of this duty of care. Reliance on the clause was held to be unreasonable and Lord Griffiths set down four factors which should always be considered in an adjudication on reasonableness and are discussed further below. These are:

- Equality of bargaining power
- Alternatives open to the customer
- The difficulty of the task for which liability is being excluded
- The practical consequences of the decision.

Lord Griffith's view of these factors is discussed below, along with other relevant authorities.

Bargaining power (see Schedule 2(a), UCTA)

In relation to bargaining power his Lordship said (at p 530):

> "Were the parties of equal bargaining power? If the court is dealing with a one-off situation between parties of equal bargaining power the requirement of reasonableness would be more easily discharged than in a case such as the present where the disclaimer is imposed on the purchaser who has no effective power to object."

It seems that the lack of bargaining may to some extent be compensated for in the eyes of the court if there has been prior bargaining over the term between a trade and consumer association.

We can see this thinking pre-UCTA in the judgment of Lord Diplock in *Schroeder Music Publishing Co Ltd* v *Macaulay* [1974] 3 All ER 616. His

SALE AND SUPPLY OF GOODS

Lordship drew a distinction between standard form contracts which had been drawn up by years of negotiation between trade bodies, and those which had been drawn up by the supplier with no input from interests representing the other party (at 624).

In *R W Green Ltd* v *Cade Bros Farms* [1978] 1 Lloyd's Rep 602 an important factor in holding a term between seed merchants and farmers to be reasonable was that it had been used for some time with the approval of bodies negotiating on behalf of the respective traders. It may also be that if bodies representing the interests of buyers could have objected to a term (but have chosen not to) this may negate the strength of the buyer's argument that he had less bargaining power than the seller (see *George Mitchell* v *Finney Lock Seeds* below).

Closely linked to bargaining strength is the issue of the clarity of the language of the term and the steps taken to draw it to the other's attention (see UCTA, Sched 2(c) above and *Knight Machinery* v *Rennie* 1995 SLT 166). Clearly if the term is not known of, or cannot be understood it cannot be bargained over.

Available alternatives (see Schedule 2(b) above)

As to available alternatives, Lord Griffiths asked (at p 530):

> "Would it have been reasonably practicable to obtain the advice from an alternative source taking into account considerations of cost and time. In the present case it is urged on behalf of the surveyor that it would have been easy for the purchaser to have obtained his own report on the condition of the house, to which the purchaser replies that he would then be required to pay twice for the same advice and that people buying at the bottom end of the market, many of whom will be young first time buyers, are likely to be under considerable financial pressure without the money to go paying twice for the same service."

If this approach is set in the context of exclusion or limitation of quality obligation and remedies in commercial contracts for the sale of goods it is likely that while a choice of terms may not be insisted upon, it would certainly improve the chances of a term being reasonable. So if a seller wishes to exclude consequential loss completely, then he should perhaps offer an alternative term (at a higher price) which allows recovery of some or all of any consequential loss.

EXEMPTION CLAUSES

Difficulty of the task
Lord Griffiths posed the question (at p 530):

> "how difficult is the task being undertaken for which liability is excluded? When a very difficult or dangerous undertaking is involved there may be a high risk of failure which would certainly be a pointer towards the reasonableness of excluding liability as a condition of doing the work. A valuation, on the other hand, should present no difficulty if the work is undertaken with reasonable skill and care. It is only defects which are observable by a careful visual examination that have to be taken into account and I cannot see that it places any unreasonable burden on the valuer to require him to accept responsibility for the fairly elementary degree of skill and care involved in observing, following up and reporting on such defects. Surely it is work at the lower end of the surveyor's field of professional expertise."

Collins makes the point (Collins, *Law of Contract*, 1993), that there is a tendency to wish to enforce duties of care. He cites *Waldron Kelly* v *BRB* [1981] 3 Cur Law 33 in which the plaintiff claimed damages for breach of contract or negligence when the defendants lost a suitcase which they were carrying for him. The defendant sought to rely upon a limitation clause which limited their liability to about a tenth of what the plaintiff claimed for. The clause was held to be unreasonable and a highly significant reason was the existence of fault on the part of the defendants within a contract in which they had greater bargaining strength, and the consumer had no realistic alternative sources of supply. In the court's view it was reasonable to expect the defendants to insure.

Suppliers of goods who are also manufacturers or who have some other control over the quality of the goods should therefore note that if they are negligent it is unlikely that an exemption clause will stand.

There are circumstances in which (despite the existence of negligence) other factors weigh sufficiently in favour of the clause to make it reasonable. It might be, for instance, that the limitation of liability is only small and/or that it is much more practical for the customer to insure, and/or that the task being carried out by the supplier is a very difficult one. In *Fred Chappell Ltd* v *NCP Ltd* (*The Times*, 9 May 1978) the judge remarked *obiter* that because it was very difficult to provide the protection for lorries using a car park, this would have weighed in favour of a exemption cause.

15

SALE AND SUPPLY OF GOODS

Practical consequences
Lord Griffiths (at pp 530-31) asked:

> "What are the practical consequences of the decisions on the question of reasonableness? This [question] must involve the sums of money potentially or stake and the ability of the parties to bear the loss involved, which, in its turn, raises the question of insurance. There was once a time when it was considered improper even to mention the possible existence of insurance cover in a lawsuit. But those days are long past. Everyone knows that all prudent professional men carry insurance, and the availability of and cost of insurance must be a relevant factor when considering which of the two parties should be required to bear the risk of a loss."

But how is it decided which party is better able to bear the loss in question? In *George Mitchell* v *Finney Lock Seeds* [1983] 2 AC 803 (concerning the supply of defective seed) it was said that is was reasonable to expect the supplier to take out insurance because it would not materially have increased the contract price of the seed which was being supplied.

Any argument that the party subject to the exemption clause should insure and allow the supplier to escape the normal liability rules must not only be assessed *vis à vis* the financial burden it would impose but also in terms of the practical difficulties involved and whether it would appropriately eradicate the risk in question. In *Phillips Products* v *Hyland* [1987] 2 All ER 620 there was a contract for the hire of a JCB and driver. One of the terms provided that the driver should be deemed to be the servant or agent of the hirer. The latter could have protected himself against this by insurance: however, there was insufficient time to do so and this weighed against the terms being held to be reasonable.

An argument that the customer could have insured may also fail because of the view that the overriding priority is for the supplier to comply with his duty of care. In *Woodman* v *Photo Trade Processing* (1981) 131 NLJ 935 it was said that:

> "The customer cannot buy a replacement photograph with his insurance moneys. What he really wants is some assurance that the processor will take extra care not to lose his more precious films."

These decisions make it clear that while section 11(4) of UCTA enjoins the court to look at party resources and the question of insurance in the case of limitation clauses, the courts regard these questions as relevant to all exemption clauses.

EXEMPTION CLAUSES

Key cases

Fred Chappell Ltd v NCP Ltd, The Times, 9 May 1978
George Mitchell v Finney Lock Seeds [1983] 2 AC 803
Green, RW, Ltd v Cade Bros Farms [1978] 1 Lloyd's Rep 602
Johnstone v Bloomsbury Health Authority [1991] 2 All ER 293
Knight Machinery v Rennie, 1995 SLT 166
Phillips Products v Hyland [1987] 2 All ER 620
R and B Customs Brokers Co Ltd v United Dominions Trust Ltd [1988] 1 All ER 847
Schroeder Music Publishing Co Ltd v Macaulay [1974] 3 All ER 616
Smith v Bush; Harris v Wyre Forest DC [1989] 2 All ER 514, HL
Waldron Kelly v BRB [1981] 3 Cur Law 33
Woodman v Photo Trade Processing (1981) 131 NLJ 935

CHAPTER 2

The Quality Obligation

Selling in the course of a business	21
The correct interpretation of section 14(1) SGA	22
The quality standard	23
How price may lower the standard	23
Importance of description	23
Fitness for purposes	24
Drawing attention to limitations on purposes	24
Use of exemption clauses	24
Buyer with uncommon purpose	25
Non-functional problems	25
Exempting liability for non-functional defects	26
Durability	26
Second hand goods	26
Defects and examination	26
Summary of exemption clauses	27
Sale by an agent in the course of a business	27
Liability of private seller acting through a business agent	27
Checklist for application of the quality obligation	30
Key cases	31

SALE AND SUPPLY OF GOODS

CHAPTER 2
The Quality Obligation

Section 1 of the Sale and Supply of Goods Act 1994 (SSGA) and other minor provisions in the schedules amend sections 14 and 15 of the Sale of Goods Act 1979 (SGA). The effect is the replacement of the merchantability standard in contracts of sale with a satisfactory quality standard. The amended section 14 reads as follows:

"14(2) Where the seller sells goods in the course of a business, there is an implied term that the goods supplied under the contract are of satisfactory quality.

(2A) For the purposes of this Act, goods are of satisfactory quality if they meet the standard that a reasonable person would regard as satisfactory, taking account of any description of the goods, the price (if relevant) and all the other relevant circumstances.

(2B) For the purposes of this Act, the quality of goods includes their state and condition and the following (among others) are in appropriate cases aspects of the quality of goods –

(a) fitness for all the purposes for which goods of the kind in question are commonly supplied;

(b) appearance and finish;

(c) freedom from minor defects;

(d) safety and

(e) durability.

(2C) The term implied by sub section (2) above does not extend to any matter making the quality of goods unsatisfactory –

(a) which is specifically drawn to the buyer's attention before the contract is made;

(b) where the buyer examines goods before the contract is made, which that examination ought to reveal, and

THE QUALITY OBLIGATION

    (c) in the case of a contract for sale by sample, which would have been apparent on a reasonable examination of the sample."

The Schedules to the SSGA 1994 amend the various pieces of legislation which apply to other contracts under which goods pass, namely hire, hire purchase and contracts for the transfer of goods. The satisfactory quality standard also now applies to all of these contracts (see Appendix III).

Selling in the course of a business

In Chapter 1 the *R & B Customs Brokers* case was discussed in which it was said that a person only *buys* in the course of a business where the purchase is integral to the business by virtue of forming part of a frequent pattern of such transactions, or representing a one-off trade venture. The same approach has been taken to *selling* in the course of a business in *Davies* v *Sumner* [1984] 1 WLR 1301 where there could only be criminal liability under the Trade Descriptions Act 1968 for false statements if the defendant was selling in the course of a business. If the same approach is taken to the satisfactory quality standard then many sales by businesses will not be covered, such as where a solicitor sells his office chairs or a baker sells his oven (unless this is a regular occurrence). On this approach buyers must be extremely vigilant at the negotiation stage. They must consider what type of business the seller is primarily in, whether he frequently deals in other products, and most importantly, what proportion of his overall business activities are taken up by the sort of transaction which is about to be undertaken. If the answer is that this type of transaction is an uncommon one for the seller then the buyer must recognise that the satisfactory quality implied term may not protect him, and that he should negotiate for an express contractual commitment on quality.

Of course it is possible that the courts would not follow the *R & B Customs* and *Davies* v *Sumner* approach in this specific context. It could be argued that the approach was taken in the *R & B Customs* case in order to ensure consumer status and therefore greater protection for the small business *buyer* as he was in that case. From one perspective the *Davies* v *Sumner* decision is more difficult to distinguish, in that it related to the issue of *selling* in the course of a business. As indicated it was held that the sale in question had to be integral to the business. However, it can be argued that this approach was taken to limit the exposure of seller to the criminal liability which arises under the Trade Description Act. Breach of the satisfactory quality standard only attracts civil liability for breach of contract. In addition it might be said that there would be an intolerable burden of enquiry upon buyers if they had to research and enquire as to the seller's business activities in the way outlined above.

It could, therefore, be argued that the courts would hold there to be a sale in the course of a business whenever there is a sale by way of trade irrespective of whether the sale is integral to the business. This approach is supported by the Law Commission's 1969 report upon which the current wording is based (see Law Com, No 24, para 31). It is also supported by the Scottish Outer House Case, *Buchanan-Jardine* v *Hamilink and Another*, 1983 SLT 149 decided under section 14(2), in which it was held that any sale of business equipment is a sale in the course of a business (Lord Dunpark at p 61).

On this approach it is sellers who must act with caution, and assume that the sale of anything related to a business being run, may be held to be a sale in the course of a business.

A business seller might try to avoid this scenario by effecting a sale to a family member or friend who is a private individual. They could then make a sale to a third party, and this would arguably escape section 14 as not being in the course of a business. There are two possible dangers associated with this strategy. First, the court might say that the family member or friend was nothing more than an agent for the business seller, who had therefore sold in the course of a business to the third party and was covered by section 14. Second, if the court did come to this conclusion then any advertisement by the agent which implied that the sale was private would probably amount to a criminal offence by the agent under the Business Advertisements (Disclosure) Order 1977 (SI 1977/1918).

The correct interpretation of section 14(1) SGA

The position is unclear and both buyers and sellers must be on their guard whenever goods are sold which are not normally traded in by the seller in question. It is submitted that the second approach is correct, however, and that a sale (as opposed to a purchase) need not be integral to a business to be in the course of a business under section 14(2). There is no direct English authority on section 14(2), and the combined weight of the Law Commission report and the Buchanan case must be highly persuasive in England. The Buchanan case is binding on lower courts in Scotland unless and until overturned by the inner House of the Court of Session or the House of Lords.

THE QUALITY OBLIGATION

It also seems that experience of selling a particular sort of product is only one reason that the law feels inclined to impose a quality obligation on business sellers. There is, in addition, the fact that business sellers are in a better position to insure themselves against the risk of liability than private sellers. Even if not actually insured they will probably find it relatively easy to absorb the loss involved in having to give a refund and pay damages.

The quality standard (see section 14 set out at p 20 above)

There is a general test in subsection 2(A) relating to the quality standard, and a list of criteria relevant to this test is set out in subsection 2(B).

The factors set out in subsection 2(B) must be read in the context of the general test: for example the fact that a product has a minor defect, (see subs 2(B)(c)) does not mean that it is necessarily of unsatisfactory quality. All relevant factors must be balanced to determine if the goods meet the standard that a reasonable person would regard as satisfactory.

Safety may be an exception to this, as it surely must be the case that goods fail the test if they are unsafe. There will be many other circumstances when products clearly fail: for example by not being able to perform their function at all, or hardly at all; as in the case of a car that rarely starts or does not start at all; a washing machine that hardly cleans clothes or not at all; or an umbrella which is full of holes or collapses constantly in the slightest wind.

How price may lower the standard

The real challenge for the test comes with the less clear cut cases, such as where the car, washing machine or umbrella in the above examples are erratic rather than nearly useless. Here the criteria in the test are really put to use. A lower than average price might indicate a lower standard, although, as Ervine has pointed out, the reduction may have been to induce a quick sale rather than to indicate inferior quality (see Ervine, "The Sale & Supply of Goods Act 1994", 1995 SLT 1). Price may have been reduced for both of these purposes (*e.g.* where meat is "reduced for quick sale" in a supermarket), and this must lower the standard such that the meat perhaps need not be as tender as otherwise. Of course it must not give the purchaser food poisoning, or it is clearly not of satisfactory quality.

Importance of description

Description (in advertising material, on packaging, in verbal negotiation etc) is also very important and can raise or lower the level that a reasonable person thinks is satisfactory. For example, a description which speaks in glowing terms of how a product has been manufactured to the highest standards of design is likely to help to make unsatisfactory a product which turns out to be erratic rather than useless.

None of the factors listed in subsection 2(B) are conclusive. However factors (a)-(c) and (e) probably go some way towards making the satisfactory quality standard higher than the merchantability standard was. Factor (d) makes no difference as products would have been unmerchantable if they were unsafe, just as they will be unsatisfactory if they are unsafe.

Fitness for purposes

Factor (a) is relevant because the idea of "fitness for purposes" is altered in two important respects from the old section 14(2). There is no longer a reference to fitness for "any of the purposes" for which such goods are commonly supplied but to fitness for "all purposes" for which such goods are commonly supplied. This means that there is less room for a seller to argue, for example, that, even although a four wheel drive does not perform well on rough terrain, at least it performs satisfactorily on the road (see *Aswan Engineering Establishment* v *Lupdine* [1987] 1 WLR 1). This position seems to give rise to three practical implications for sellers at the contracting stage.

First of all they may wish to exercise a high degree of care in their quality management processes to ensure that goods are fit for all of their common purposes. The implications of this will clearly vary depending upon the range of purposes which are common for any given product. This is something which should be seriously reflected upon. If a product can be and is commonly used for a wide range of purposes then the seller must consider whether it is fit for all of these purposes.

Drawing attention to limitations on purposes

A second possibility for sellers is to draw the buyer's attention to specific limitations which might affect the usefulness of the product for certain purposes which happen to be common purposes. This will prevent the obligation from being owed in this respect (see 2(C)(a) above) and mean that buyers are more fully informed as to exactly what they can expect from the goods in question. This process should be built in to contracting procedures.

Use of exemption clauses

A third consideration for sellers will be whether they can use an exemption clause, or increase the scope of any exemption clause already in use, as a

THE QUALITY OBLIGATION

means of limiting the impact of any increase in the primary quality obligation which they may now face. Such a clause could either:

- reduce the scope of the primary obligation, for example, by saying that the goods need only be suitable for certain specific purposes or for the most common purposes, and/or,
- reduce the amount of damages payable by reference to weight, contract price etc.

This might be done in respect of breach of the primary obligation in general, or in respect of a particular breach (*e.g.* lack of usefulness for certain sorts of purposes). Of course such possibilities are only available where the buyer is not a consumer (see UCTA ss 6, 7, 12, 20, 21, and 25) and where the term can be shown to be reasonable (see UCTA ss 11, 24 and Chap 1 above). As we have said in Chapter 1, exemptions are most likely to be reasonable where they are clearly expressed and disclosed (see *Knight Machinery* and Sched 2(c) above); where they have been the subject of some negotiation between trade bodies, or where the parties are of equal bargaining strength (Sched 2(a), *RW Green* v *Cade Bros*); where the buyer is offered an alternative term which does not exempt the obligation or liability to the same degree (*Woodman* v *Photo Trade Processing*, Sched 2(b)) and where the buyer is better able to insure against the particular risk allocation in question (*George Mitchell* v *Finney Lock Seed*, *Phillips* v *Hyland*, s 11(4)).

Buyer with uncommon purpose
If the buyer has a purpose in mind which is not "common" at all (*e.g.* to inflate hot water bottles with his lungs as part of a strongman act) then failure to fulfill this purpose is unlikely to make the goods unsatisfactory. In such a case a buyer should make his purpose known and he may have a remedy under section 14(3) if the goods do not make the grade.

Non-functional problems
The reference to "appearance and finish" 2(B)(b) and "freedom from minor defects" 2(B)(c) is important because it emphasises that the standard is concerned with factors other than the functionality of the product. This had been in doubt in the case of the old definition due to the decisions in cases such as *Millar's of Falkirk* v *Turpie* 1976 SLT 66. However the case of *Rogers* v *Parish (Scarborough) Ltd* [1987] 2 ALL ER 232 seemed to confirm that even the old definition required that at least a new (in this case) car should be capable of being driven "with the appropriate degree of comfort, ease of handling and reliability and ... of pride in the vehicle's outward and

interior appearance" (Mustill LJ). We now have statutory confirmation of this, which is useful for a buyer because it enables him to point to this criteria on the list of factors in 2B and press home his claim to the seller.

Exempting liability for non-functional defects

Once again sellers in commercial contracts might use an exemption clause to water down the primary obligation, saying, for example, that the product is only of unsatisfactory quality where it is functionally defective. Alternatively, they might limit or exclude the remedies available in the case of non functional defects (see comments above about the approach of the courts to the UCTA reasonableness test).

Durability

The inclusion of durability as a criteria is probably most important from the point of view of emphasis. The old definition apparently required that goods be durable in the sense that they be in such a state at the time of the delivery that they will last for a reasonable amount of time (see *Lambert* v *Lewis* [1982] AC 225, and Ervine, "Durability, Consumers and the Sale of Goods Act", 1984 JR 147). However, buyers tended to be uncertain on this point, and this uncertainty could easily be exploited by sellers, especially against consumer buyers with a very limited understanding of their rights (see on this point and on the background to the new law, Willett, "The Unacceptable Face of the Consumer Guarantees Bill", 54 MLR 552, and Willett, "The Quality of Goods and the Rights of Consumers", 44 NILQ 218). Sellers in commercial sales could attempt to exempt liability in respect of lack of durability (see comments on exemption clauses above).

Second hand goods

The standard for second hand goods will clearly be lower than for new goods, as the price will be less and there will be more of an expectation of minor defects. An important measure of comparison (as with new goods) will be how the goods in question compare to comparable goods in a similar market at a similar price. The worse the comparison, the more likely it is that the goods will be unsatisfactory.

Defects and examination

Turning now to section 14 2(C), two points are of importance. First, paragraph (a) means defects *specifically* pointed out. It is no good for a seller to get a buyer to sign or acknowledge a statement that says "all defects are acknowledged", or "all non-functional defects are acknowledged", or something akin to this. If a seller is to be excused from a particular defect that would make the goods unsatisfactory in whatever respect he

THE QUALITY OBLIGATION

must point that defect out. Secondly, the buyer need not examine goods but if he does he must find what a reasonable person would find, (*i.e.* what the examination ought to reveal) otherwise he cannot complain.

Summary of exemption clauses

The use of exemption clauses in commercial contracts as a means of limiting or excluding certain aspects of the primary obligation or limiting or excluding the remedies available to the buyer for breach of certain elements of the primary obligation have been discussed above. The primary obligation might be watered down in any number of ways *e.g.* by saying that goods need only be fit for some purposes, or that goods need only be functional, not aesthetically perfect, nor free from minor defects. As to remedies, there might be a term which limits the liability of the seller in damages to direct losses and excludes consequential loss. There might also be a term which excludes or limits the right to reject. Again, of course such terms are subject to the UCTA reasonableness test (see ss 6, 7, 11, 20, 21 and 24 of UCTA).

Sale by an agent in the course of a business

Section 14 of the Sale of Goods Act (and the equivalent provisions for hire purchase, hire and transfer, contained in the Sale of Goods (Implied Terms) Act 1973 and the Supply of Goods and Services Act 1982) also contains important rules on the application of the quality standard in cases where the sale is by an agent. The fundamental question is when a sale through a business agent involves the principal (who would otherwise be a private seller, not selling in the course of a business) being covered by section 14 (and the equivalent provisions applying to other contracts for the supply of goods). The issue is dealt with by section 14(5) (and equivalent provisions for other contracts involving the supply of goods). Section 14(5) reads as follows.

> "The preceding provisions of this section apply to a sale by a person who in the course of business is acting as agent for another as they apply to a sale by a principal in the course of a business, except where that other is not selling in the course of a business and either the buyer knows that fact or reasonable steps are taken to bring it to the notice of the buyer before the contract is made."

Liability of private seller acting through a business agent

Although this section might have been worded slightly more clearly the intention seems to be to impose the quality obligation on private sellers where they sell through a business agent, unless the buyer knows that the seller is not selling in the course of a business or reasonable steps are taken to draw this to his attention.

The beginning of the section speaks of its application to a sale by a person who in the course of business is acting as an agent to another. A sale by such a person (or any agent) will be a sale to a buyer involving a contract between the principal and the buyer, so it is the liability of the principal with which the subsection is concerned. This liability will exist, according to the remainder of the subsection, unless the buyer knows the seller is private, or steps have been taken to point this out. In other words the buyer who buys from a business agent is entitled to assume that the principal is acting in the course of a business.

It seems that this is the effect which the Law Commission would have wished to achieve. In the *First report on exemption clauses* (1969, Law Com No 24 and Scot Law Com No 12) it was pointed out that sales by private parties were not covered by the implied terms even where there was a business agent (*e.g.* an auctioneer) on whose reputation the buyer might rely when deciding whether to purchase. The idea was that if a person chooses to take the advantages of selling through a business agent, then there should be a quid pro quo. A greater reliance on reputation, skill, judgment etc will have been made by the buyer on the business agent than could reasonably have been made upon a private seller who was selling directly to a buyer. At the same time the agent is not a party to the contract of sale and so cannot bear an implied term type obligation; although he could be liable in tort or delict if he made statements which were fraudulent, or which were negligent and in respect of which a duty of care could be established.

It has been confirmed in the recent House of Lords decision of *Boyter* v *Thomson* [1995] 3 All ER 135 that section 14(5) covers all situations in which a sale is carried out through a business agent, not merely those cases in which there is an undisclosed principal. The defender was the owner of a cabin cruiser and he instructed Harbour Marine & Leisure of Kircaldy to sell it on his behalf. The pursuer bought the boat and later discovered various defects rendering her unseaworthy. These amounted to breaches of the obligation of quality, and that of fitness for purpose. The pursuer took action against the defender, arguing that he owed the various implied obligations, by virtue of section 14(5). It was argued by the defender that section 14(5) did not operate to impose the relevant obligations upon the defender, as it only applied to the obligations owed by agents where they acted for an undisclosed principal.

THE QUALITY OBLIGATION

This argument was rejected by Lord Jauncey on behalf of the remainder of the House (Lords Lloyd, Nolan, Nicholls and Hoffman). It was correctly pointed out that the second part of the sub-section (beginning with "except") clearly presupposed that there could be liability outside situations where there was an undisclosed principal, otherwise it would be superfluous to speak of the buyer's knowledge of whether the principal was selling in the course of a business. How could a buyer ever be aware of this if he did not even know of the existence of the principal?

The lesson for private sellers (whether private individuals, or businesses which in the context of the sale in question are not acting in the course of a business) seems to be twofold. First, they must take steps, themselves or via the agent, to ensure that prospective buyers are aware that they are not selling in the course of a business. A business must be particularly vigilant here because if a court later says that a sale in the course of a business took place (under s 14(1)) then the business will have committed an offence if they have used an advertisement to say that the sale is private (Business Advertisements (Disclosure) Order 1977). In other words this tactic should only be used where the principal is genuinely private and not acting in the course of a business under section 14(1).

The other tactic which can be employed is to use a clause excluding or limiting any liability which does arise. Such a clause would be controllable by the UCTA in the context of contracts of sale and hire purchase even in cases where the principal does not sell in the course of a business but is only covered by section 14(2) due to section 14(5). This is because in the case of sale and hire purchase exclusion or restriction of the implied terms is controllable even where the sale is not in the course of a business (see ss 6(4) and 20). This means that an exclusion or limitation would be of no effect in a consumer sale, and would be subject to the reasonableness test in a commercial sale. As usual terms are more likely to be reasonable if they are clear in their language and clearly disclosed, if the breach of the obligation has not been caused by the negligence of the seller, if the buyer is best placed to insure, and if a choice is offered between a limited and a full liability service (see Chap 1).

In other contracts for the transfer of goods (*e.g.* hire, work and materials) the UCTA controls only apply where the contract was in the course of a business (ss 1(3) and 21(3)). So private suppliers who do not sell in the course of a business but who use a business agent and are therefore liable under section 14(5) are probably free of UCTA controls, and can exempt liability.

SALE AND SUPPLY OF GOODS

Checklist for application of the quality obligation

Is sale or supply in course of a business? (probably including any sale of business equipment)

If *yes* then the quality obligation applies

Test of "satisfactory quality", which takes account of:

- *descriptions* in advertisements, packaging, negotiations
- *price* (average market price implies average market quality)
- *fitness for all common purposes*
- *appearance and finish*
- *freedom from minor defects*
- *safety*
- *durability*

Possible use of exemption clauses in commercial contracts to

(a) exclude entire obligation, or
(b) exclude a part of the obligation *e.g.* in respect of minor defects
(c) exclude or limit the damages and/or the right to reject if there is a breach of the obligation.

Obligation will not apply:

(a) where specific defects pointed out
(b) where buyer examines and should have found the defect (s) in question.

Quality obligation may apply to private seller, selling through business agent.

THE QUALITY OBLIGATION

Key cases

Aswan Engineering Establishment v Lupdine [1987] 1 WLR 1
Boyter v Thomson [1995] 3 All ER 135
Buchanan-Jardine v Hamilink and Another 1983 SLT 149
Davies v Sumner [1984] 1 WLR 1301
Lambert v Lewis [1982] AC 255
Millar's of Falkirk v Turpie 1976 SLT 66
R and B Customs Brokers Co Ltd v United Dominions Trust Ltd [1988] 1 All ER 847
Rogers v Parish (Scarborough) Ltd [1987] 2 All ER 232

CHAPTER 3

Remedies

Right to reject for breach of contract: introduction	34
Slight or immaterial breaches	34
"Reasonableness and the right to reject"	35
Contracting out of the rules on slight and immaterial breaches	35
Loss of right to reject by acceptance	36
Acceptance by intimation	38
Acceptance by inconsistent act	38
Acceptance by lapse of reasonable time	39
Exemption clauses to exclude or limit the right to reject	40
Right of partial rejection	41
Buyer's choice as to termination?	41
Damages	43
Setting off losses against the price	44
Exemption clauses to exclude or limit buyer's right to damages	45
Summary of remedies	45
Key cases	46

SALE AND SUPPLY OF GOODS

CHAPTER 3

Remedies

Right to reject for breach of contract: introduction

In English law the previous position was that any breach of the implied terms gave both consumer and commercial buyers a right to reject the goods and terminate the contract (s 11 SGA). The position in Scotland was less clear, but in both Scotland and England the position is now that a consumer buyer can always reject and terminate for breach of one of the implied terms (SGA ss 11 and 15 B (2))[1]. However, the rules on rejection for commercial buyers have been changed so that they can only reject in England where the breach is not so slight as to make rejection unreasonable, and in Scotland where the breach is material (SGA, s 15 B). Where the buyer is a consumer the breach is always deemed to be material (s 15(B)(2)). These amendments to the SGA were made by ss 4 and 5 of the Sale and Supply of Goods Act 1994.

Slight or immaterial breaches

What counts as a breach which is so slight as to make it unreasonable to reject the goods? The situation will depend on the sort of term which has been broken. When dealing with the satisfactory quality term it may be, for example, that if the stereo system in a new company car is not working then it is not of satisfactory quality, although this may be a breach which is so slight as to make it unreasonable to reject. It seems clear that for a breach to be "slight" it is going to have to be very small in proportion to the whole contract.

The contrast between the English and Scottish tests is interesting. In England the breach must be "slight" and the seller must prove this. In Scotland on the other hand, the buyer has no right to reject unless he (the buyer) can establish that the breach is material. The buyer in England is clearly in the better position that the buyer in Scotland where a relatively minor breach is concerned. Such a breach may well not be material: materiality of breach occurs where the degree of breach is fairly serious. It

[1] Subject to the rules on acceptance – see below.

must also be remembered that it is for the buyer in Scotland to prove this serious breach. However, in an English court the seller will often be unable to establish that a breach is slight in nature. Indeed not only must the breach be slight in England if the buyer is to lose his right to reject, it must be so slight that it would be unreasonable for him to reject.

"Reasonableness and the right to reject"

It is important to give a proper reading to the idea of unreasonableness in the new section 15 A. It is not enough that the breach be slight. It must make rejection unreasonable, as it often will. However, it will not always do so: for example there may be a slight breach, which is nevertheless fatal to the usefulness of the goods, or which the seller refuses to acknowledge or negotiate over, causing inconvenience for the buyer. In such circumstances it may be perfectly reasonable to reject.

The issue is whether the slightness of the breach pulls strongly enough in favour of rejection being unreasonable to defeat whatever factors there are which suggest that rejection is reasonable. It is here that we see a good faith principle in operation and working both ways. On the one hand the law is trying to protect the seller against rejection for very slight breaches. On the other hand the seller must surely respond positively to the buyer's complaints, and to requests for cure. If he does not then it may be that it is perfectly reasonable for the buyer to reject for a slight breach. After all it is surely unreasonable to reject for a slight breach, mainly because the seller should be given the chance to make amends in some other way (*e.g.* by a reduction in price, or by repair), and also because it is hard to explain the buyer's unwillingness to give the seller this opportunity other than by concluding that the buyer is rejecting for some bad faith reason (*e.g.* because the market circumstances have made it attractive to escape the bargain).

If the buyer has given the seller a chance to cure and the seller is uncooperative then it may be more reasonable for the buyer to reject even where the breach is slight. Of course the English buyer need only rely on reasons as to why it is reasonable to reject where the breach is very slight. Anything more than a slight breach, and no reason other than the existence of the breach is needed.

Contracting out of the rules on slight and immaterial breaches

In both England and Scotland it is open to the parties to agree that the rules as to slight and immaterial breaches do not apply (ss 15A(2) and 15B(2)). It is interesting to question the applicability of s 3(2)(b)(1) of the

UCTA to an English *buyer's* terms, which give him or her the right to reject for any breach, however slight. Section 3(2)(b)(1) says that any term contained in a party's written standard terms that offers a contractual performance substantially different from that which was reasonably expected is subject to the reasonableness test. Can it be said that a term giving the right to reject for a very minor breach offers a contractual performance substantially different from what was reasonably expected by the seller?[2] If it can, then the term would be subject to the reasonableness test. As usual the very least required to make such a term reasonable would be that it is clear in its import (see discussion above in Chap 1).

It is slightly less clear as to whether the Scottish equivalent of UCTA section 3(2)(b) (UCTA s 17(1)(b)) can apply to a *buyer's* terms. Under section 17(1)(b) the term is only subject to the reasonableness test where it is offering a contractual performance substantially different from what his *customer* reasonably expected. So this section can only apply to a buyer's terms if a seller can be regarded as a buyer's "customer" in the context of a buyer's obligations to accept and pay for the goods. This is not an impossible conclusion to reach, but does seem to be out of step with the normal understanding of "customer".

Loss of right to reject by acceptance

In contracts of sale the buyer is seemed to have "accepted" goods when he intimates to the seller that he has accepted them, or when the goods have been delivered to him and he does any act in relation to them which is inconsistent with the ownership of the seller, or when, after the lapse of a reasonable time, he retains the goods without intimating to the seller that he has rejected them (s 35, Sale of Goods Act 1979, as amended by s 2 Sale & Supply of Goods Act 1994). Once the buyer has accepted the goods he loses the right to reject. This is quite independent of the above rules as to slight and immaterial breaches which only apply to commercial buyers. Both consumer and commercial buyers can lose the right to reject by acceptance. In other supply contracts the right to reject can be lost by buyers subject to common law rules which are of similar effect to the acceptance rules although slightly more generous to buyers.

The key at common law is doctrine of affirmation. The buyer loses the right to reject by affirming the contract. However, he cannot affirm the

---

[2] The commercial context and past dealings between the parties would surely have a large role in determining what it is reasonable to expect as far as rejection for slight defects is concerned.

REMEDIES

contract until he knows of any defects (see *Farnworth Finance* v *Attryde* [1970] 2 All ER 774). As shown below there can be acceptance under the SGA without knowledge of the defect. We will focus here on the Sale of Goods Act acceptance rules. The new section 35 reads:

"(1) The buyer is deemed to have accepted the goods subject to subsection (2) below –

  (a) when he intimates to the seller that he has accepted them, or

  (b) when the goods have been delivered to him and he does any act in relation to them which is inconsistent with the ownership of the seller.

(2) Where goods are delivered to the buyer, and he has not previously examined them, he is not deemed to have accepted them under subsection (1) above until he has had a reasonable opportunity of examining them for the purpose –

  (a) of ascertaining whether they are in conformity with the contract, and

  (b) in the case of a contract for sale by sample, of comparing the bulk with the sample.

(3) Where the buyer deals as consumer or (in Scotland) the contract of sale is a consumer contract, the buyer cannot lose his right to reply on subsection (2) above by agreement, waiver or otherwise.

(4) The buyer is also deemed to have accepted the goods when after the lapse of a reasonable time he retains the goods without intimating to the seller that he has rejected them.

(5) The questions that are material in determining for the purposes of subsection (4) above whether a reasonable time has elapsed include whether the buyer has had a reasonable opportunity of examining the goods for the purpose mentioned in subsection (2) above.

(6) The buyer is not by virtue of this section deemed to have accepted the goods merely because –

  (a) he asks for, or agrees to, their repair by or under an arrangement with the seller, or

  (b) the goods are delivered to another under a sub-sale or other disposition."

Acceptance by intimation

Acceptance by intimation will normally involve some form of express indication by the purchaser that he is happy with the goods, or perhaps an implied indication such as the inspection of goods over a short period, followed by the sending of a payment. An important issue in the context of acceptance by intimation is whether the signature of some type of formal "acceptance note" involves acceptance by intimation. Clearly if the buyer has drafted the note himself then this is the most obvious form of acceptance by intimation. The problem, however, comes with the sort of note that the seller has drafted and presented to the buyer. The basic question is, of course, what counts as "intimation" and whether the buyer is really intimating anything in such circumstances.

It seems that the particular circumstances will be crucial and the courts will be interested in whether the note represents the real substance of what has happened—*i.e.* the real intentions of the buyer. This appears to be more likely the case where the note is plain and intelligible in its language, where the buyer is given a clear opportunity to consider it, and where the contents of the note involve some form of acknowledgement of the buyer being happy with the goods and awareness that he is not entitled to reject them. What is absolutely clear is that there cannot be acceptance by intimation until the buyer has a reasonable opportunity of examining the goods to ascertain whether they are in conformity with the contract (see s 35(2) above). This means that any formal signature which is obtained before the buyer has seen or had the chance to examine the goods could never amount to acceptance by intimation.

So if a seller wishes to ensure that there is acceptance under this heading he should draft the acceptance note in such a way that it is not only in plain language but also clearly involves an acknowledgement of loss of the right to reject. The seller should also ensure that he has offered an opportunity for examination before presenting the acceptance note to the buyer.

Acceptance by inconsistent act

There could be acceptance by inconsistent act, such as where the buyer destroys or defaces the goods. Depending upon the circumstances and commercial context it might be that a sub-sale of goods by the buyer would amount to acceptance by an inconsistent act. There might also be negotiations between the seller and buyer which involve commitments on both sides, for example to carry out a repair or contribute to certain costs etc. It is possible that these or other circumstances might, on the facts, involve an act by the buyer inconsistent with the ownership of the seller. It must be stressed, however, that the facts of each case must be considered. Section 35(6) makes it clear that there is no acceptance of any kind simply because the buyer agrees to a repair, or the buyer effects a sub-sale of the goods. This is significant because there has always been the likelihood that sellers would argue that agreeing to a repair or effecting a sub-sale in themselves amounted to acceptance by inconsistent act. It is now clear that whether they do or not depends on the facts of each case. It seems likely that the courts would pay close attention to commercial practice in deciding what actions of a commercial buyer are inconsistent with the ownership of the seller.

Buyers should be aware of this when they first take possession of goods, and should generally be wary of how they treat goods while they are ascertaining their suitability. Against this, there cannot be acceptance under this heading until there has been a reasonable opportunity for examination (s 35(2)).

Acceptance by lapse of reasonable time

What amounts to a "reasonable time" will vary depending on the particular circumstances and commercial context. It may be that there are understandings between traders as to how long buyers have to check out goods. In the absence of such factors the type of products will be important. The courts are likely to be reluctant to allow a very long period where the goods are very expensive and the seller will find himself in a state of insecurity as to whether he will have to refund money.

In the English case of *Bernstein* v *Pamson Motors* [1987] 2 All ER 135 the Court of Appeal held that there had been lapse of a reasonable time when a car was not rejected for three weeks, despite the fact that the defect had only manifested itself at this stage. The court in the Bernstein case placed some stress on the importance of commercial certainty and the seller being able to "close the ledger". Little account was taken of the fact that it was probably not reasonable to have expected the buyer to have discovered the defect before he did. However, the new section 35 made an important change to the reasonable time rule, which may tip the balance slightly in favour of buyers. Section 35(5) says that:

> "The questions that are material in determining ... whether a reasonable time has elapsed include whether the buyer had a reasonable opportunity of examining the goods [to ascertain that they conform to the contract]"

This should mean that buyers are in a stronger position where a latent defect is concerned. It must be emphasised that the opportunity to examine is not a precondition of loss of the right to reject as it is under the other two headings. It is rather a factor in considering whether a reasonable time has lapsed. At the same time this is only one balancing factor, and it might still be argued that commercial certainty should take precedence in the circumstances (see discussion in Willett, 44 NILQ 218 at 221-23).

It is submitted that the introduction of the examination issue as an explicit criteria must mean that it should be given a higher profile in the overall test than was done in *Bernstein*. The courts should therefore place a reasonable degree of significance on whether there was a reasonable opportunity to discover the defect.

The Scottish courts have always tended to take a more buyer-friendly view to the reasonable time rule. They have tended to place emphasis upon the nature of the defect and whether it was reasonable to expect the buyer to have discovered it (see *Hyslop* v *Shirlaw* (1905) 7F 875, and discussions in Willett and O'Donnell, *Scottish Business Law*, 2nd ed, (1996) 440-442).

Exemption clauses

A seller in a commercial contract will be able to exclude or limit the right to reject if it is reasonable to do so (ss 6, 7, 11, 13, UCTA). In deciding upon reasonableness the courts will look especially at the width of the exclusion (*i.e.* the degree to which the right to reject is limited or excluded), along with:

- how clear the term is
- whether it has ever been negotiated over by trade bodies
- whether the buyer had a choice of another term which did not exclude or limit the remedy in question
- and who is regarded as being best placed to insure against the risk in question (see generally Chap 1 above).

REMEDIES

Right of partial rejection

If some of the goods in a non-severable contract of sale are defective section 11(4) of the Sale of Goods Act says that the buyer cannot rely on this breach of condition to reject some of the goods and accept others. However this rule has now been made subject to the new section 35 A (introduced by s 3 of the 1994 Act). Under this new provision the buyer does not lose his right to reject some of the goods because he has accepted others in the consignment so long as he has accepted all of those which are not defective (s 35(A)(1)). The same provisions are made regarding instalments of goods under the new section 35A(2).

The rules on partial rejection are subject to the provisions regarding commercial units in section 35(7) (inserted by s 2 of the 1994 Act) which say that where the contract is for the sale of goods making one or more commercial units, a buyer accepting any goods in a unit is deemed to have accepted all the goods making the unit. In this subsection "commercial unit" means a unit the division of which would materially impair the value of the goods, or the character of the unit.

In contracts of supply other than sale, as has already been said, the buyer's rights to reject are affected by common law "affirmation" rules, meaning that the right to reject can only be lost when there is knowledge of the defect. This point apart the courts would be likely to apply an analogous approach to partial rejection to that taken by the Sale of Goods Act as described above.

Buyer's choice as to termination?

The constraints which may exist on the buyer's right to reject for breach of contract have been discussed above. If this right to reject arises, the buyer also has the right to terminate the contract.

However, the buyer need not exercise the right to terminate. He may simply reject, and give the opportunity to the seller to cure the defect, by repair or replacement. On exercising this option the buyer is keeping the contract alive (see discussion by Bradgate [1995] Cons LJ 94 at 103-4).

All of the above discussions have involved the situation where the seller is actually in breach of contract. However, it is arguable that if the seller delivers defective goods before the time for the final performance then although the buyer has a right to reject the goods, the seller can insist upon curing and retendering before the final date for performance unless his defective tender is very serious and the buyer can treat the contract as repudiated. The buyer's right to reject defective goods before the contractual date for performance is not based on a breach of contract because as yet there has been no such breach. The buyer is entitled to reject under section 27 of the Sale of Goods Act which says that:

> "It is the duty of the seller to deliver the goods, and of the buyer to accept and pay for them, in accordance with the terms of the contract of sale."

It can be argued that these duties are interdependent, so that if the seller does not deliver "in accordance with the terms of the contract of sale" the buyer need not accept the goods. If the seller delivers goods which are defective then they are not in accordance with the terms, one of which says that they must be of satisfactory quality. This does not necessarily mean that there is an actual breach of a condition of the contract, and there is clear support for this proposition in at least one judgment. In *Smith* v *Wheatsheaf Mills Ltd* [1939] 2 KB 302 Branson J said that:

> "It cannot be said that the seller becomes in breach the moment he tenders goods which for some reason or other (it may be for some purely formal reason with regard to the documents) they buyer can say are not in fulfilment of the contract, and the seller cannot put himself right by making a subsequent tender" (at p 315).

There is also support for this approach in an extra-judicial statement by Lord Devlin.

> "A tender of a ship (or of goods under a contract for the sale of goods) in a condition that does not comply with the terms of the contract is not a breach of contract. What creates the breach in such a case is the failure to tender within the contact time[goods] in a condition that does comply with the contract" (1966) CLJ 192 at p 194.

In other words up until the contract time has expired it can be argued that there is no breach of contract giving rise to a right to reject *and* terminate but simply a failure to provide goods which accord with the contract giving a right to reject only. The seller can therefore re-tender. The obvious practical advice for sellers is to do this before the time for performance has expired.

There is an interesting question in relation to the buyer's right to reject defective goods before the due date of tender. As already said, this is not based on the existence of a breach of contract but on the principle that a buyer need not accept goods which do not conform with the contract (see s 27 above). There seems to be no reason why a buyer should be prevented from rejecting the goods in these circumstances even where the quality defect is very slight or (in Scotland) where the defect is not material. This is because the controls in sections 15 A and B on rejecting in such circumstances are restricted to the right to reject **and terminate for breach of contract** (see above). If there has been no breach of contract then these sections do not apply. It might, of course, be argued that the reference to breach in sections 15 A and B includes anticipatory breach. However even if it does it is hard to see how (in England) a slight or (in Scotland) a non-material breach represents an intention on the part of the buyer not to perform. If it does not then there is no anticipatory breach.

In further support of the commercial buyer's right to reject for slight or immaterial breaches before the time for performance, it might be argued that the buyer has a legitimate interest in trying (up until the performance date) to get the seller to tender goods which conform precisely. At this stage this may be what he is using his power of rejection for. At the breach stage, the slight/immaterial breach rules are justified in particular because a right to terminate is available along with the right to reject, and this seems a very harsh burden for the seller to bear for small breaches. Before there is a breach of contract the buyer can only reject: he cannot terminate the contract.

The courts might apply a good faith or legitimate interest rule to the buyer who rejects a seller's early tender but who knows that it is impossible for the seller to improve on this tender. Therefore it might be said that there could not be rejection in such a case due to lack of good faith on the part of the buyer, or the lack of a legitimate interest in rejection.

Damages

In contracts for the sale of goods there is specific provision for damages for breach of the implied terms as to description, quality and fitness for purpose. Section 53(2) says that the "measure of damages ... is the estimated loss directly and naturally resulting, in the ordinary course of events, from the breach ..." This reflects the general position in contract law, and is indeed modelled upon the first part of the rule in *Hadley* v *Baxendale* (1854) 9 Exch 341.

Section 53(3) goes on to provide a particular model for calculating losses where there is a breach of the quality obligation,

"... such loss is prima facie the difference between the value of the goods at the time of delivery to the buyer and the value they would have had if they had [not been in breach of the quality obligation]."

This allows for recovery of the basic loss suffered due to the product not being worth what was paid for it. The buyer may also be able to claim special damages for loss of the profits which would have been made on a resale, if this was foreseeable. There can also be a claim for any loss of further orders which results from the buyer's inability to fulfil his sub-sale (see *GKN Centrax Gears Ltd* v *Matbro Ltd* [1976] 2 Lloyds Rep 555 CA); or as a means of indemnifying the buyer against a claim brought against him by his sub-buyer (see *Godley* v *Perry* [1960] 1 WLR 9.

There may also be a claim for loss of profits which would have been earned from the use of the goods (*George Mitchell* v *Finney Lock Seeds*), for damage caused by the defective goods to the buyer's other property and for personal injury. A consumer will be able to claim disappointment damages.

As always the claims are subject to rules on remoteness of damage, and to the buyer's duty to mitigate his losses.

Setting off losses against the price

Section 53(1) of the Sale of Goods Act allows the buyer to set up the breach of the quality obligation "in diminution or extinction of the price". This enables the buyer to exercise the "self help" remedy of withholding the price. If the seller sues for the price the buyer can then set up the breaches of contract as a means for reducing or extinguishing his liability. If the buyer's damages exceed the price he could then bring a separate action to recover these damages. Alternatively this could be done in the form of a counterclaim to the seller's claim for the price.

Although it will often happen in practice it is less clear whether, in strict theory, there can be a set-off in other contracts for the supply of goods. This is because it could be seen as an exercise of the *actio quanti minoris* (an action for the reduction of price) which is not generally recognised in either Scots or English law. Given that remedies for breach of the quality obligation in these other contracts is governed by common law rules and not the Sale of Goods Act it is likely that the right to set off the buyer's loss against price does not exist.

REMEDIES

Exemption clauses to exclude or limit buyer's right to damages

Sellers to commercial buyers can exclude or limit the buyer's right to damages if it is reasonable to do so (ss 6, 7, 11, 13, 24, 25 and Sched 2 UCTA). Outright or almost outright exclusions of the buyer's right to damages are unlikely to be successful (see *George Mitchell* v *Finney Lock Seeds*). Whatever degree of exemption is adopted, terms are most likely to be reasonable if clearly expressed and if a choice of some kind was offered to the buyer. An exemption is likely to be unreasonable if the seller is thought best placed to insure or has been negligent (see Chap 1).

Summary of remedies

Rejection
Consumer
Always available (subject to acceptance or affirmation rules)

Commercial buyers
Breach must not be so slight as to make rejection unreasonable. In Scotland breach must be material. Even then, subject to acceptance rules.

Damages
Consumer & commercial buyers
1. Can claim for:
   - reduction in value
   - loss of profits on resale
   - liabilities to sub-buyers
   - loss of profits due to inability to put to intended use
   - damage to property
   - injury
   - disappointment (only consumers)

2. Losses must not be too remote.

3. Must mitigate losses.

Reduction of price
   - Possible under s 53(1) of SGA.

SALE AND SUPPLY OF GOODS

Key cases

Bernstein v Pamson Motors [1987] 2 All ER 220, CA
Farnworth Finance v Attryde [1970] 2 All ER 774
GKN Centrax Gears Ltd v Matbro Ltd [1976] 2 Lloyd's Rep 555, CA
Hadley v Baxendale (1854) 9 Exch 341
Hyslop v Shirlaw (1905) 7F 875
Smith v Wheatsheaf Mills Ltd [1939] 2 KB 302
Woodman v Photo Trade Processing (1981) 131 NLP 935

APPENDIX I

Appendix I

Relevant Provisions of the Unfair Contract Terms Act 1977

Sections 6, 7, 11, 12, 13 and Schedule 2

6. Sale and hire-purchase
(1) Liability for breach of the obligations arising from—

(a) [section 12 of the Sale of Goods Act 1979] (seller's implied undertakings as to title etc.);

(b) section 8 of the Supply of Goods (Implied Terms) Act 1973 (the corresponding thing in relation to hire-purchase),

cannot be excluded or restricted by reference to any contract term.

(2) As against a person dealing as consumer, liability for breach of the obligations arising from—

(a) [section 13, 14, or 15 of the 1979 Act] (seller's implied undertakings as to conformity of goods with description or sample, or as to their quality of fitness for a particular purpose);

(b) section 9, 10 or 11 of the 1973 Act (the corresponding thing in relation to hire-purchase),

cannot be excluded or restricted by reference to any contract term.

(3) As against a person dealing otherwise than as consumer, the liability specified in subsection (2) above can be excluded or restricted by reference to a contract term, but only in so far as the term satisfies the requirement of reasonableness.

(4) The liabilities referred to in this section are not only the business liabilities defined by section 1 (3), but include those arising under any contract of sale of goods or hire-purchase agreement.

7. Miscellaneous contracts under which goods pass
(1) Where the possession or ownership of goods passes under or in pursuance of a contract not governed by the law of sale of goods or hire-purchase, subsections (2)

SALE AND SUPPLY OF GOODS

to (4) below apply as regards the effect (if any) to be given to contract terms excluding or restricting liability for breach of obligation arising by the implication of law from the nature of the contract.

(2) As against a person dealing as consumer, liability in respect of the goods correspondence with description or sample, or their quality or fitness for any particular purpose, cannot be excluded or restricted by reference to any such term.

(3) As against a person dealing otherwise than as consumer, that liability can be excluded or restricted by reference to such a term, but only in so far as the term satisfies the requirement of reasonableness.

[(3A) Liability for breach of the obligations arising under section 2 of the Supply of Goods and Services Act 1982 (implied terms about title etc. in certain contracts for the transfer of the property in goods) cannot be excluded or restricted by reference to any such term.]

(4) Liability in respect of—

(a) the right to transfer ownership of the goods, or give possession; or

(b) the assurance of quiet possession to a person taking goods in pursuance of the contract,

cannot [in a case to which subsection (3A) does not apply] be excluded or restricted by reference to any such term except in so far as the term satisfies the requirement of reasonableness.

(5) This section does not apply in the case of goods passing on a redemption of trading stamps within the Trading Stamps Act 1964 or the Trading Stamps Act (Northern Ireland) 1965.

Explanatory provisions

11. The 'reasonableness' test

(1) In relation to a contract term the requirement of reasonableness for the purposes of this Part of this Act, section 3 of the Misrepresentation Act 1967 and section 3 of the Misrepresentation Act (Northern Ireland) 1967 is that the term shall have been a fair and reasonable one to be included having regard to the circumstances which were, or ought reasonably to have been, known to or in the contemplation of the parties when the contract was made.

(2) In determining for the purposes of section 6 or 7 above whether a contract term satisfies the requirement of reasonableness, regard shall be had in particular to the matters specified in Schedule 2 to this Act; but this subsection does not prevent the

APPENDIX I

court or arbitrator from holding, in accordance with any rule of law, that a term which purports to exclude or restrict any relevant liability is not a term of the contract.

(3) In relation to a notice (not being a notice having contractual effect), the requirement of reasonableness under this Act is that it should be fair and reasonable to allow reliance on it, having regard to all the circumstances obtaining when the liability arose or (but for the notice) would have arisen.

(4) Where by reference to a contract term or notice a person seeks to restrict liability to a specified sum of money, and the question arises (under this or any other Act) whether the term or notice satisfies the requirement of reasonableness, regard shall be had in particular (but without prejudice to subsection (2) above in the case of contract terms) to—

- (a) the resources which he could expect to be available to him for the purpose of meeting the liability should it arise; and
- (b) how far it was open to him to cover himself by insurance.

(5) It is for those claiming that a contract term or notice satisfies the requirement of reasonableness to show that it does.

12. 'Dealing as consumer'

(1) A party to a contract 'deals as consumer' in relation to another party if—

- (a) he neither makes the contract in the course of a business nor holds himself out as doing so; and
- (b) the other party does make the contract in the course of a business; and
- (c) in the case of a contract governed by the law of sale of goods or hire-purchase, or by section 7 of this Act, the goods passing under or in pursuance of the contract are of a type ordinarily supplied for private use or consumption.

(2) But on a sale by auction or by competitive tender the buyer is not in any circumstances to be regarded as dealing as consumer.

(3) Subject to this, it is for those claiming that a party does not deal as consumer to show that he does not.

13. Varieties of exemption clause

(1) To the extent that this Part of this Act prevents the exclusion or restriction of any liability it also prevents—

- (a) making the liability or its enforcement subject to restrictive or onerous conditions;

(b) excluding or restricting any right to remedy in respect of the liability, or subjecting a person to any prejudice in consequence of his pursuing any such right or remedy;

(c) excluding or restricting rules of evidence or procedure;

and (to that extent) sections 2 and 5 to 7 also prevent excluding or restricting liability by reference to terms and notices which exclude or restrict the relevant obligation or duty.

(2) But an agreement in writing to submit present or future differences to arbitration is not to be treated under this Part of this Act as excluding or restricting any liability.

Schedule 2 Guidelines for Application of Reasonableness Test

Sections 11(2) and 24(2)
The matters to which regard is to be had in particular for the purposes of sections 6(3), 7(3) and (4), 20 and 21 are any of the following which appear to be relevant—

(a) the strength of the bargaining positions of the parties relative to each other, taking into account (among other things) alternative means by which the customer's requirements could have been met;

(b) whether the customer received an inducement to agree to the term, or in accepting it had an opportunity of entering into a similar contract with other persons, but without having top accept a similar term;

(c) whether the customer knew or ought reasonably to have known of the existence and extent of the term (having regard, among other things, to any custom of the trade and any previous course of dealing between the parties);

(d) where the term excludes or restricts any relevant liability if some condition is not complied with, whether it was reasonable at the time of the contract to expect that compliance with that condition would be practicable;

(e) whether the goods were manufactured, processed or adapted to the special order of the customer.

Appendix II

Previous Legislative Provisions: Sale of Goods Act 1979 Sections 11, 14, 15, 30, 34, 35

11. When condition to be treated as warranty

(1) Subsections (2) to (4) and (7) below do not apply to Scotland and subsections (5) below applies only to Scotland.

(2) Where a contract of sale is subject to a condition to be fulfilled by the seller, the buyer may waive the condition, or may elect to treat the breach of the condition as a breach of warranty and not as a ground for treating the contract as repudiated.

(3) Whether a stipulation in a contract of sale is a condition, the breach of which may give rise to a right to treat the contract as a repudiated, or a warranty, the breach of which may give rise to a claim for damages but not to a right to reject the goods and treat the contract as repudiated, depends in each case on the construction of the contract; and a stipulation may be a condition, though called a warranty in the contract.

(4) Where a contract of sale is not severable and the buyer has accepted the goods or part of them, the breach of a condition to be fulfilled by the seller can only be treated as a breach of warranty, and not as a ground for rejecting the goods and treating the contract as repudiated, unless there is an express or implied term of the contract to that effect.

(5) In Scotland, failure by the seller to perform any material part of a contract of sale is a breach of contract, which entitles the buyer either within a reasonable time after delivery to reject the goods and treat the contract as repudiated, or to reject the goods and treat the failure to perform such material just as a breach which may give rise to a claim for compensation or damages.

(6) Nothing in this section affects a condition or warranty whose fulfilment is excused by law by reason of impossibility or otherwise.

(7) Paragraph 2 of Schedule 1 below applies in relation to a contract made before 22 April 1967 or (in the application of this Act to Northern Ireland) 28 July 1967.

SALE AND SUPPLY OF GOODS

14. Implied terms about quality or fitness

(1) Except as provided by this section and section 15 below and subject to any other enactment, there is no implied condition or warranty about the quality or fitness for any quality or fitness, particular purpose of goods supplied under a contract of sale.

(2) Where the seller sells goods in the course of a business, there is an implied condition that the goods supplied under the contract are of merchantable quality, except that there is no such condition:-

   (a) as regards defects specifically drawn to the buyer's attention before the contract is made; or

   (b) if the buyer examines the goods before the contract is made, as regards defects which that examination ought to reveal.

(3) Where the seller sells goods in the course of a business and the buyer, expressly or by implication, makes known:-

   (a) to the seller; or

   (b) where the purchase price or part of it is payable by instalments and the goods were previously sold be a credit broker to the seller, to that credit broker,

   any particular purpose for which the goods are being bought, there is an implied condition that the goods supplied under the contract are reasonably fit for that purpose, whether or not that is a purpose for which such goods are commonly supplied, except where the circumstances show that the buyer does not rely, or that it is unreasonable for him to rely, on the skill or judgement of the seller or credit broker.

(4) An implied condition or warranty about quality or fitness for a particular purpose may be annexed to a contract of sale by usage.

(5) The preceding provisions of this section apply to a sale by a person who in the course of a business is acting as agent for another as they apply to a sale by a principal in the course of a business except where that other is not selling in the course of a business and either the buyer knows that fact or reasonable steps are taken to bring it to the notice of the buyer before the contract is made.

(6) Goods of any kind are of merchantable quality within the meaning of subsection (2) above if they are as fit for the purpose or purposes for which goods of that kind are commonly bought as it is reasonable to expect having regard to any description applied to them, the price (if relevant) and all the other relevant circumstances.

(7) Paragraph 5 of Schedule 1 below applies in relation to a contract made on or after 18 May 1973 and before the appointed day and paragraph 6 in relation to one made before 18 May 1973.

(8) In subsection (7) above and paragraph 5 of Schedule 1 below references to the appointed day are to the day appointed for the purposes of those provisions by an order of the Secretary of State made by statutory instrument.

15. Sale by sample
(1) A contract of sale is a contract for sale by sample sale by where there is an express or implied term to that effect in the sample contract.

(2) In the case of a contract for sale by sample there is an implied condition:-

(a) that the bulk will correspond with the sample in quality;

(b) that the buyer will have a reasonable opportunity of comparing the bulk with the sample

(c) that the goods will be free from any defect, rendering them unmerchantable, which would not be apparent on reasonable examination of the sample.

(3) In subsection (2)(c) above "unmerchantable" is to be construed in accordance with section 14(6) above.

(4) Paragraph 7 of Schedule 1 below applies in relation to a contract made before 18 May 1973.

30. Delivery of wrong quantity
(1) Where the seller delivers to the buyer a quantity of goods less than he contracted to sell, the buyer may reject them, but if the buyer accepts the goods so delivered he must pay for them at the contract rate.

(2) Where the seller delivers to the buyer a quantity of goods larger than he contracted to sell, the buyer may accept the goods included in the contract and reject the rest, or he may reject the whole.

(3) Where the seller delivers to the buyer a quantity of goods larger than he contracted to sell and the buyer accepts the whole of the goods so delivered he must pay for them at the contract rate.

(4) Where the seller delivers to the buyer the goods he contracted to sell mixed with goods of a different description not included in the contract, the buyer may accept the goods which are in accordance with the contract and reject the rest, or he may reject the whole.

SALE AND SUPPLY OF GOODS

(5) This section is subject to any usage of trade, special agreement, or course of dealing between the parties.

34. Buyer's right of examining the goods

(1) Where goods are delivered to the buyer, and he has not previously examined them, he is not deemed to have accepted them until he has had a reasonable opportunity of examining them for the purpose of ascertaining whether they are in conformity with the contract.

(2) Unless otherwise agreed, when the seller tenders delivery of goods to the buyer, he is bound on request to afford the buyer a reasonable opportunity of examining the goods for the purpose of ascertaining whether they are in conformity with the contract.

35. Acceptance

(1) The buyer is deemed to have accepted the goods when he intimates to the seller that he has accepted them, or (except where section 34 above otherwise provides) when the goods have been delivered to him and he does any action in relation to them which is inconsistent with the ownership of the seller, or when after the lapse of a reasonable time he retains the goods without intimating to the seller that he has rejected them.

Appendix III

Text of the Sale and Supply of Goods Act 1994

1994 CHAPTER 35

An Act to amend the law relating to the sale of goods; to make provision as to the terms to be implied in certain agreements for the transfer of property in or the hire of goods, in hire-purchase agreements and on the exchange of goods for trading stamps and as to the remedies for breach of the terms of such agreements; and for connected purposes. [3rd November 1994]

Be it enacted by the Queen's most excellent Majesty, by and with the advice and consent of the Lords Spiritual and Temporal, and Commons, in the present Parliament assembled, and by the authority of the same, as follows:—

Provisions relating to the United Kingdom

1. Implied term about quality

(1) In section 14 of the Sale of Goods Act 1979 (implied terms about quality or fitness) for subsection (2) there is substituted—

'(2) Where the seller sells goods in the course of a business, there is an implied term that the goods supplied under the contract are of satisfactory quality.

(2A) For the purposes of this Act, goods are of satisfactory quality if they meet the standard that a reasonable person would regard as satisfactory, taking account of any description of the goods, the price (if relevant) and all the other relevant circumstances.

(2B) For the purposes of this Act, the quality of goods includes their state and condition and the following (among others) are in appropriate cases aspects of the quality of goods—

    (a) fitness for all the purposes for which goods of the kind in question are commonly supplied,

    (b) appearance and finish,

(c) freedom from minor defects,

(d) safety, and

(e) durability.

(2C) The term implied by subsection (2) above does not extend to any matter making the quality of goods unsatisfactory—

(a) which is specifically drawn to the buyer's attention before the contract is made,

(b) where the buyer examines the goods before the contract is made, which that examination ought to reveal, or

(c) in the case of a contract for sale by sample, which would have been apparent on a reasonable examination of the sample.

(2) In section 15 of that Act (sale by sample) in subsection (2)(c) for 'rendering them unmerchantable' there is substituted 'making their quality unsatisfactory'.

2. Acceptance of goods and opportunity to examine them

(1) In section 35 of the Sale of Goods Act 1979 (acceptance) for the words from 'when he intimates' to '(2)' there is substituted—

'subject to subsection (2) below —

(a) when he intimates to the seller that he has accepted them, or

(b) when the goods have been delivered to him and he does any act in relation to them which is inconsistent with the ownership of the seller.

(2) Where goods are delivered to the buyer, and he has not previously examined them, he is not deemed to have accepted them under subsection (1) above until he has had a reasonable opportunity of examining them for the purpose—

(a) of ascertaining whether they are in conformity with the contract, and

(b) in the case of a contract for sale by sample, of comparing the bulk with the sample.

(3) Where the buyer deals as consumer or (in Scotland) the contract of sale is a consumer contract, the buyer cannot lose his right to rely on subsection (2) above by agreement, waiver or otherwise.

(4) The buyer is also deemed to have accepted the goods when after the lapse of a reasonable time he retains the goods without intimating to the seller that he has rejected them.

(5) The questions that are material in determining for the purposes of subsection (4) above whether a reasonable time has elapsed include whether the buyer has had a reasonable opportunity of examining the goods for the purpose mentioned in subsection (2) above.

(6) The buyer is not by virtue of this section deemed to have accepted the goods merely because—

(a) he asks for, or agrees to, their repair by or under an arrangement with the seller, or

(b) the goods are delivered to another under a sub-sale or other disposition.

(7) Where the contract is for the sale of goods making one or more commercial units, a buyer accepting any goods included in a unit is deemed to have accepted all the goods making the unit; and in this subsection 'commercial unit' means a unit division of which would materially impair the value of the goods or the character of the unit.

(8)'.

(2) In section 34 of that Act (buyer to have opportunity to examine goods)—

(a) the words from the beginning to '(2)' are repealed; and

(b) at the end of that section there is inserted 'and, in the case of a contract for sale by sample, of comparing the bulk with the sample.'

3. Right of partial rejection

(1) After section 35 of the Sale of Goods Act 1979 there is inserted the following section—

'35A. Right of partial rejection

(1) If the buyer—

(a) has the right to reject the goods by reason of a breach on the part of the seller that affects some or all of them, but

(b) accepts some of the goods, including, where there are any goods unaffected by the breach, all such goods,

he does not be accepting them lose his right to reject the rest.

(2) In the case of a buyer having the right to reject an instalment of goods, subsection (1) above applies as if references to the goods were references to the goods comprised in the instalment.

(3) For the purposes of subsection (1) above, goods are affected by a breach if by reason of the breach they are not in conformity with the contract.

(4) This section applies unless a contrary intention appears in, or is to be implied from the contract.'

(2) At the beginning of section 11(4) of that Act (effect of accepting goods) there is inserted 'Subject to section 35A below'.

(3) Section 30(4) of that Act (rejection of goods not within contract description) is repealed.

Provisions relating to England and Wales and Northern Ireland

4. Modification of remedies in non-consumer cases

(1) After section 15 of the Sale of Goods Act 1979 there is inserted the following—

'Miscellaneous

15A Modification of remedies for breach of condition in non-consumer cases

(1) Where in the case of a contract of sale—

(a) the buyer would, apart from this subsection, have the right to reject goods by reason of a breach on the part of the seller of a term implied by section 13, 14 or 15 above, but

(b) the breach is so slight that it would be unreasonable for him to reject them,

then, if the buyer does not deal as consumer, the breach is not to be treated as a breach of condition but may be treated as a breach of warranty.

(2) This section applies unless a contrary intention appears in, or is to be implied from the contract.

(3) It is for the seller to show that a breach fell within subsection (1)(b) above.

(4) This section does not apply to Scotland.'

APPENDIX III

(2) In section 30 of that Act (delivery of shortfall or excess) after subsection (2) there is inserted—

'(2A) A buyer who does not deal as consumer may not—

(a) where the seller delivers a quantity of goods less than he contracted to sell, reject the goods under subsection 1 above, or

(b) where the seller delivers a quantity of goods larger than he contracted to sell, reject the whole under subsection (2) above,

if the shortfall or, as the case may be, the excess is so slight that it would be unreasonable for him to do so.

(2B) It is for the seller to show that a shortfall or excess fell within subsection (2A) above.

(2C) Subsections (2A) and (2B) above do not apply to Scotland.'

Provisions relating to Scotland

5. Remedies for breach of contract

(1) After section 15A of the Sale of Goods Act 1979, which is inserted by section 4(1) above, there is inserted the following section—

'15B. Remedies for breach of contract as respects Scotland

(1) Where in a contract of sale the seller is in breach of any term of the contract (express or implied), the buyer shall be entitled—

(a) to claim damages, and

(b) if the breach is material, to reject any goods delivered under the contract and treat it as repudiated.

(2) Where a contract of sale is a consumer contract, then, for the purposes of subsection (1)(b) above, breach by the seller of any term (express or implied)—

(a) as to the quality of the goods or their fitness for a purpose,

(b) if the goods are, or are to be, sold by description, that the goods will correspond with the description,

(c) if the goods are, or are to be, sold by reference to a sample, that the bulk will correspond with the sample in quality,

shall be deemed to be a material breach.

(3) This section applies to Scotland only.'

(2) In section 30 of that Act (delivery of shortfall or excess) before subsection (3) there is inserted—

'(2D) Where the seller delivers a quantity of goods—

(a) less than he contracted to sell, the buyer shall not be entitled to reject the goods under subsection (1) above,

(b) larger than he contracted to sell, the buyer shall not be entitled to reject the whole under subsection (2) above,

unless the shortfall or excess is material.

(2E) Subsection (2D) above applies to Scotland only.'

(3) After section 53 of that Act there is inserted the following section—

'53A. Measure of damages as respects Scotland
(1) The measure of damages for the seller's breach of contract is the estimated loss directly and naturally resulting, in the ordinary course of events, from the breach.

(2) Where the seller's breach consists of the delivery of goods which are not of the quality required by the contract and the buyer retains the goods, such loss as aforesaid is prima facie the difference between the value of the goods at the time of delivery to the buyer and the value they would have had if they had fulfilled the contract.

(3) This section applies to Scotland only.'

6. Provision equivalent to Part I of Supply of Goods and Services Act 1982
Schedule 1 to this Act shall have effect for the purpose of making provision equivalent to Part I of the Supply of Goods and Services Act 1982 for Scotland.

General

7. Amendments and repeals
(1) Schedule 2 to this Act (which makes minor and consequential amendments of the Sale of Goods Act 1979 and the Uniform Laws on International Sales Act 1967, and makes amendments of enactments relating to the supply of goods corresponding to the amendments of that Act of 1979 made by this Act) shall have effect.

(2) The enactments mentioned in Schedule 3 to this Act are repealed to the extent specified in column 3 of that Schedule.

APPENDIX III

8. Short title, commencement and extent

(1) This Act may be cited as the Sale and supply of Goods Act 1994.

(2) This Act shall come into force at the end of the period of two months beginning with the day on which it is passed.

(3) This Act has effect in relation to contracts of sale of goods, hire purchase agreements, contracts for the transfer of goods, contracts for the hire of goods and redemptions of trading stamps for goods (as the case may be) made after this Act comes into force.

(4) This Act extends to Northern Ireland.

SCHEDULES

SCHEDULE 1 PROVISION EQUIVALENT TO PART I OF SUPPLY
OF GOODS AND SERVICES ACT 1982
FOR SCOTLAND

Section 6

1. After Part I of the Supply of Goods and Services Act 1982 there is inserted the following Part—

'PART 1A SUPPLY OF GOODS AS RESPECTS SCOTLAND

Contracts for the transfer of property in goods

11A. The contracts concerned

(1) In this Act in its application to Scotland a "contract for the transfer of goods" means a contract under which one person transfers or agrees to transfer to another the property in goods, other than an excepted contract.

(2) For the purposes of this section an excepted contract means any of the following—

(a) a contract of sale of goods;

(b) a hire-purchase agreement;

(c) a contract under which the property in goods is (or is to be) transferred in exchange for trading stamps on their redemption;

(d) a transfer or agreement to transfer for which there is no consideration;

(e) a contract intended to operate by way of mortgage, pledge, charge or other security.

SALE AND SUPPLY OF GOODS

(3) For the purposes of this Act in its application to Scotland a contract is a contract for the transfer of goods whether or not services are also provided or to be provided under the contract, and (subject to subsection (2) above) whatever is the nature of the consideration for the transfer or agreement to transfer,

11B. Implied terms about title, etc.

(1) In a contract for the transfer of goods, other than one to which subsection (3) below applies, there is an implied term on the part of the transferor that in the case of a transfer of the property in the goods he has a right to transfer the property and in the case of an agreement to transfer the property in the goods he will have such a right at the time when the property is to be transferred.

(2) In a contract for the transfer of goods, other than one to which subsection (3) below applies, there is also an implied term that—

(a) the goods are free, and will remain free until the time when the property is to be transferred, from any charge or encumbrance not disclosed or known to the transferee before the contract is made, and

(b) the transferee will enjoy quiet possession of the goods except so far as it may be disturbed by the owner or other person entitled to the benefit or any charge or encumbrance so disclosed or known.

(3) This subsection applies to a contract for the transfer of goods in the case of which there appears from the contract or is to be inferred from its circumstances an intention that the transferor should transfer only such title as he or a third person may have.

(4) In a contract to which subsection (3) above applies there is an implied term that all charges or encumbrances known to the transferor and not known to the transferee have been disclosed to the transferee before the contract is made.

(5) In a contract to which subsection (3) above applies there is also an implied term that none of the following will disturb the transferee's quiet possession of the goods, namely—

(a) the transferor;

(b) in a case where the parties to the contract intend that the transferor should transfer only such title as a third person may have, that person;

(c) anyone claiming through or under the transferor or that third person otherwise than under a charge or encumbrance disclosed or known to the transferee before the contract is made.

(6) In section 21 of the 1977 after subsection (3) there is inserted the following subsection—

"(3A) Notwithstanding anything in the foregoing provisions of this section, any term of a contract which purports to exclude or restrict liability for breach of the obligations arising under section 11B of the Supply of Goods and Services Act 1982 (implied terms about title, freedom from encumbrances and quiet possession in certain contracts for the transfer of property in goods) shall be void."

11C. Implied terms where transfer is by description

(1) This section applies where, under a contract for the transfer of goods, the transferor transfers or agrees to transfer the property in the goods by description.

(2) In such a case there is an implied term that the goods will correspond with the description.

(3) If the transferor transfers or agrees to transfer the property in the goods by reference to a sample as well as by description it is not sufficient that the bulk of the goods corresponds with the sample if the goods do not also correspond with the description.

(4) A contract is not prevented from falling within subsection (1) above by reason only that, being exposed for supply, the goods are selected by the transferee.

11D. Implied terms about quality or fitness

(1) Except as provided by this section and section 11E below and subject to the provisions of any other enactment, there is no implied term about the quality or fitness for any particular purpose of goods supplied under a contract for the transfer of goods.

(2) Where, under such a contract, the transferor transfers the property in goods in the course of a business, there is an implied term that the goods supplied under the contract are of satisfactory quality.

(3) For the purposes of this section and section 11E below, goods are of satisfactory quality if they meet the standard that a reasonable person would regard as satisfactory, taking account of any description of the goods, the price (if relevant) and all the other relevant circumstances.

(4) The term implied by subsection (2) above does not extend to any matter making the quality of goods unsatisfactory—

SALE AND SUPPLY OF GOODS

(2) For the purposes of this section, an excepted contract means any of the following—

(a) a hire-purchase agreement;

(b) a contract under which goods are (or are to be) hired in exchange for trading stamps on their redemption.

(3) For the purposes of this Act in its application to Scotland a contract is a contract for the hire of goods whether or not services are also provided or to be provided under the contract, and (subject to subsection (2) above) whatever is the nature of the consideration for the hire or agreement to hire.

11H.   Implied terms about right to transfer possession etc.

(1) In a contract for the hire of goods there is an implied term of the part of the supplier that—

(a) in the case of a hire, he has a right to transfer possession of the goods by way of hire for the period of the hire; and

(b) in the case of an agreement to hire, he will have such a right at the time of commencement of the period of the hire.

(2) In a contract for the hire of goods there is also an implied term that the person to whom the goods are hired will enjoy quiet possession of the goods for the period of the hire except so far as the possession may be disturbed by the owner or other person entitled to the benefit of any charge or encumbrance disclosed or known to the person to whom the goods are hired before the contract is made.

(3) The preceding provisions of this section do not affect the right of the supplier to repossess the goods under an express or implied term of the contract.

11I.   Implied terms where hire is by description

(1) This section applies where, under a contract for the hire of goods, the supplier hires or agrees to hire the goods by description.

(2) In such a case there is an implied term that the goods will correspond with the description.

(3) If under the contract the supplier hires or agrees to hire the goods by reference to a sample as well as by description it is not sufficient that the bulk of the goods corresponds with the sample if the goods do not also correspond with the description.

APPENDIX III

(4) A contract is not prevented from falling within subsection (1) above by reason only that, being exposed for supply, the goods are selected by the person to whom the goods are hired.

11J. Implied terms about quality or fitness

(1) Except as provided by this section and section 11K below and subject to the provisions of any other enactment, there is no implied term about the quality or fitness for any particular purpose of goods hired under a contract for the hire of goods.

(2) Where, under such a contract, the supplier hires goods in the course of a business, there is an implied term that the goods supplied under the contract are of satisfactory quality.

(3) For the purposes of this section and section 11K below, goods are of satisfactory quality if they meet the standard that a reasonable person would regard as satisfactory, taking account of any description of the goods, the consideration for the hire (if relevant) and all the other relevant circumstances.

(4) The term implied by subsection (2) above does not extend to any matter making the quality of goods unsatisfactory—

(a) which is specifically drawn to the attention of the person to whom the goods are hired before the contract is made, or

(b) where that person examines the goods before the contract is made, which that examination ought to reveal; or

(c) where the goods are hired by reference to a sample, which would have been apparent on reasonable examination of the sample.

(5) Subsection (6) below applies where, under a contract for the hire of goods, the supplier hires goods in the course of a business and the person to whom the goods are hired, expressly or by implication, makes known—

(a) to the supplier in the course of negotiations conducted by him in relation to the making of the contract; or

(b) to a credit-broker in the course of negotiations conducted by that broker in relation to goods sold by him to the supplier before forming the subject matter of the contract,

any particular purpose for which the goods are being hired.

(6) In that case there is (subject to subsection (7) below) an implied term that the goods supplied under the contract are reasonably fit for that purpose, whether or not that is a purpose for which such goods are commonly supplied.

(7) Subsection (6) above does not apply where the circumstances show that the person to whom the goods are hired does not rely, or that it is unreasonable for him to rely, on the skill or judgment of the hirer or credit-broker.

(8) An implied term about quality or fitness for a particular purpose may be annexed by usage to a contract for the hire of goods.

(9) The preceding provisions of this section apply to a hire by a person who in the course of a business is acting as agent for another as they apply to a hire by a principal in the course of a business, except where that other is not hiring in the course of a business and either the person to whom the goods are hired knows that fact or reasonable steps are taken to bring it to that person's notice before the contract concerned is made.

11K. Implied terms where hire is by sample

(1) This section applies where, under a contract for the hire of goods, the supplier hires or agrees to hire the goods by reference to a sample.

(2) In such a case there is an implied term—

(a) that the bulk will correspond with the sample in quality; and

(b) that the person to whom the goods are hired will have a reasonable opportunity of comparing the bulk with the sample; and

(c) that the goods will be free from any defect, making their quality unsatisfactory, which would not be apparent on reasonable examination of the sample.

(3) For the purposes of this section a supplier hires or agrees to hire goods by reference to a sample where there is an express or implied term to that effect in the contract concerned.

Exclusion of implied terms, etc.

11L. Exclusion of implied terms etc.

(1) Where a right, duty or liability would arise under a contract for the transfer of goods or a contract for the hire of goods by implication of law, it may (subject to subsection (2) below and the 1977 Act) be negatived or varied by express agreement, or by the course of dealing between the parties, or by such usage as binds both parties to the contract.

(2) An express term does not negative a term implied by the preceding provisions of this Part of this Act unless inconsistent with it.

APPENDIX III

(3) Nothing in the preceding provisions of this Part of this Act prejudices the operation of any other enactment or any rule of law whereby any term (other than one relating to quality or fitness) is to be implied in a contract for the transfer of goods or a contract for the hire of goods.'

2. In section 18(1) of that Act—

(a) in paragraph (b) of the definition of 'credit-brokerage' after 'bailment' there is inserted 'or as regards Scotland the hire';

(b) in the definition of 'goods'—

(i) for 'include all personal chattels (including' there is substituted 'includes all personal chattels, other than things in action and money, and as regards Scotland all corporeal moveables; and in particular "goods" includes';

(ii) for 'or bailment' there is substituted 'bailment or hire';

(iii) '), other than things in action and money' is omitted.

3. In section 18(2) of that Act after 'assignment' there is inserted 'assignation'.

4. In section 20(6) of that Act after 'Act" there is inserted 'except Part IA, which extends only to Scotland' and for 'but not' there is substituted 'and Parts I and II do not extend'.

SCHEDULE 2 MINOR AND CONSEQUENTIAL AMENDMENTS

Section 7

The Trading Stamps Act 1964 (c. 71)

1.—(1) Section 4 of the Trading Stamps Act 1964 (terms to be implied on redemption of trading stamps) is amended as follows.

(2) In subsection (1)(a) and (b) for 'warranty' there is substituted 'term' and for subsection (1)(c) there is substituted—

'(c) an implied term that the goods are of satisfactory quality.'

(3) For subsection (2) and (3) there is substituted—

'(2) For the purposes of paragraph (c) of subsection (1) of this section, goods are of satisfactory quality if they meet the standard that a reasonable person would regard as satisfactory, taking account of any description of the goods and all the other relevant circumstances.

SALE AND SUPPLY OF GOODS

(2A) For the purposes of that paragraph, the quality of goods includes their state and condition and the following (among others) are in appropriate cases aspects of the quality of goods—

(a) fitness for all the purposes for which goods of the kind in question are commonly supplied.

(b) appearance and finish,

(c) freedom from minor defects,

(d) safety, and

(e) durability.

(2B) The term implied by that paragraph does not extend to any matter making the quality of goods unsatisfactory—

(a) which is specifically drawn to the attention of the person obtaining the goods before or at the time of redemption, or

(b) where that person examines the goods before or at the time of redemption, which that examination ought to reveal.

(3) As regards England and Wales, the terms implied by subsection (1) of this section are warranties.'

The Trading Stamps Act (Northern Ireland) 1965 (c. 6 (NI))

2.—(1) Section 4 of the Trading Stamps Act (Northern Ireland) 1965 (warranties to be implied on redemption of trading stamps) is amended as follows.

(2) For subsection (1)(c) there is substituted—

'(c) an implied warranty that the goods are of satisfactory quality.'

(3) For subsection (2) there is substituted—

'(2) For the purposes of paragraph (c) of subsection (1), goods are of satisfactory quality if they meet the standard that a reasonable person would regard as satisfactory, taking account of any description of the goods and all the other relevant circumstances.

(3) For the purpose of that paragraph, the quality of goods includes their state and condition and the following (among others) are in appropriate cases aspects of the quality of goods—

(a) fitness for all the purposes for which goods of the kind in question are commonly supplied,

APPENDIX III

(b) appearance and finish,

(c) freedom from minor defects,

(d) safety, and

(e) durability.

(4) The warranty implied by that paragraph does not extend to any matter making the quality of goods unsatisfactory—

(a) which is specifically drawn to the attention of the person obtaining the goods before or at the time of redemption, or

(b) where that person examines the goods before or at the time of redemption, which that examination ought to reveal.'

The Uniform Laws on International Sales Act 1967 (c. 45)

3. In section 1 of the Uniform Laws on International Sales Act 1967 (application of Uniform Law on the International Sale of Goods) in subsection (4)(c) for '12 to 15' there is substituted '12 to 15B'.

The Supply of Goods (Implied Terms) Act 1973 (c. 13)

4.—(1) The Supply of Goods (Implied Terms) Act 1973 is amended as follows:

(2) In section 8 (implied terms as to title)—

(a) for 'condition' (in subsection (1)(a)) and for 'warranty' (in subsections (1)(b), (2)(a) and (2)(b)) there is substituted 'term'; and

(b) at the end of that section there is inserted—

'(3) As regards England and Wales and Northern Ireland, the term implied by subsection (1)(a) above is a condition and the terms implied by subsections (1)(b), (2)(a) and (2)(b) above are warranties.'

(3) In section 9 (bailing or hiring by description)—

(a) in subsection (1) for 'condition' there is substituted 'term'; and

(b) after that subsection there is inserted—

'(1A) As regards England and Wales and Northern Ireland, the term implied by subsection (1) above is a condition.'

(4) In section 10 (implied undertakings as to quality or fitness)—

(a) for subsection (2) there is substituted—

'(2) Where the creditor bails or hires goods under a hire purchase agreement in the course of a business, there is an implied term that the goods supplied under the agreement are of satisfactory quality.

(2A) For the purposes of this Act, goods are of satisfactory quality if they meet the standard that a reasonable person would regard as satisfactory, taking account of any description of the goods, the price (if relevant) and all the other relevant circumstances.

(2B) For the purposes of this Act, the quality of goods includes their state and condition and the following (among others) are in appropriate cases aspects of the quality of goods—

    (a) fitness for all the purposes for which goods of the kind in question are commonly supplied,

    (b) appearance and finish,

    (c) freedom from minor defects,

    (d) safety, and

    (e) durability.

(2C) The term implied by subsection (2) above does not extend to any matter making the quality of goods unsatisfactory—

    (a) which is specifically drawn to the attention of the person to whom the goods are bailed or hired before the agreement is made,

    (b) where that person examines the goods before the agreement is made, which that examination ought to reveal, or

    (c) where the goods are bailed or hired by reference to a sample, which would have been apparent on a reasonable examination of the sample';

(b) for 'condition or warranty' (in subsections (1) and (4)) and for 'condition' (in subsection (3)) there is substituted 'term'; and

(c) after subsection (6) there is inserted—

'(7) As regards England and Wales and Northern Ireland, the terms implied by subsections (2) and (3) above are conditions.'

(5) In section 11 (samples)—

APPENDIX III

(a) at the beginning there is inserted '(1)';

(b) for 'condition' there is substituted 'term';

(c) in paragraph (c) for 'rendering them unmerchantable' there is substituted 'making their quality unsatisfactory'; and

(d) at the end there is inserted—

'(2) As regards England and Wales and Northern Ireland, the term implied by subsection (1) above is a condition.'

(6) After that section there is inserted the following section—

'11A. Modification of remedies for breach of statutory condition in non-consumer cases
(1) Where in the case of a hire-purchase agreement—

(a) the person to whom goods are bailed would, apart from this subsection, have the right to reject them by reason of a breach on the part of the creditor of a term implied by section 9, 10 or 11(1)(a) or (c) above, but

(b) the breach is so slight that it would be unreasonable for him to reject them,

then, if the person to whom the goods are bailed does not deal as consumer, the breach is not to be treated as a breach of condition but may be treated as a breach of warranty.

(2) This section applies unless a contrary intention appears in, or is to be implied from, the agreement.

(3) It is for the creditor to show—

(a) that a breach fell within subsection (1)(b) above, and

(b) That the person to whom the goods were bailed did not deal as consumer.

(4) The references in this section to dealing as consumer are to be construed in accordance with Part I of the Unfair Contract Terms Act 1977.

(5) This section does not apply to Scotland.'

(7) For section 12 (exclusion of implied terms and conditions) there is substituted the following section—

SALE AND SUPPLY OF GOODS

'12. Exclusion of implied terms

An express term does not negative a term implied by this Act unless inconsistent with it.;

(8) After section 12 there is inserted the following section—

'12A. Remedies for breach of hire-purchase agreement as respects Scotland

(1) Where in a hire-purchase agreement the creditor is in breach of any term of the agreement (express or implied), the person to whom the goods are hired shall be entitled—

(a) to claim damages, and

(b) if the breach is material, to reject any goods delivered under the agreement and treat it as repudiated.

(2) Where a hire-purchase agreement is a consumer contract, then, for the purposes of subsection (1) above, breach by the creditor of any term (express or implied)—

(a) as to the quality of the goods or their fitness for a purpose,

(b) if the goods are, or are to be, hired by description, that the goods will correspond with the description,

(c) if the goods are, or are to be, hired by reference to a sample, that the bulk will correspond with the sample in quality,

shall be deemed to be a material breach.

(3) In subsection (2) above "consumer contract" has the same meaning as in section 25(1) of the Unfair Contract Terms Act 1977; and for the purposes of that subsection the onus of proving that a hire-purchase agreement is not to be regarded as a consumer contract shall lie on the creditor.

(4) This section applies to Scotland only.'

(9) In section 15 (supplementary)—

(a) in subsection (1), from '"condition" and "warranty"' to 'material to the agreement' are omitted;

(b) subsection (2) is omitted; and

(c) in subsection (4), for 'condition or warranty' there is substituted 'term'.

APPENDIX III

The Sale of Goods Act 1979 (c. 54)

5.—(1) The Sale of Goods Act 1979 is amended as follows.

(2) In section 11 (when condition to be treated as warranty)—

(a) for subsection (1) there is substituted—

'(1) This section does not apply to Scotland.'; and

(b) subsection (5) is omitted.

(3) In section 12 (implied terms about title etc.)—

(a) for 'condition' (in subsection (1)) and for 'warranty' (in subsections (2), (4) and (5)) there is substituted 'term'; and

(b) after subsection (5) there is inserted—

'(5A) As regards England and Wales and Northern Ireland, the term implied by subsection (1) above is a condition and the terms implied by subsections (2), (4) and (5) above are warranties.'

(4) In section 13 (sale by description)—

(a) in subsection (1) for 'condition' there is substituted 'term'; and

(b) After that subsection there is inserted—

'(1A) As regards England and Wales and Northern Ireland, the term implied by subsection (1) above is a condition.'

(5) In section 14 (implied terms about quality or fitness)—

(a) for 'condition or warranty' (in subsections (1) and (4)) and for 'condition' (in subsection (3)) there is substituted 'term'; and

(b) for subsection (6) there is substituted—

'(6) As regards England and Wales and Northern Ireland, the terms implied by subsections (2) and (3) above are conditions.'

(6) In section 15 (sale by sample)—

(a) in subsection (2), for 'condition' there is substituted 'term' and paragraph (b) is omitted; and

(b) for subsection (3) there is substituted—

'(3) As regards England and Wales and Northern Ireland, the term implied by subsection (2) above is a condition.'

(7) In section 53 (remedy for breach of warranty) for subsection (5) there is substituted—

'(5) This section does not apply to Scotland.'

(8) In section 55 (exclusion of implied terms) in subsection (2) for 'condition or warranty' (in both places) there is substituted 'term'.

(9) In section 61 (interpretation)—

(a) in subsection (1)—

(i) after the definition of 'buyer' there is inserted—

'"consumer contract" has the same meaning as in section 25(1) of the Unfair Contract Terms Act 1977; and for the purposes of this Act the onus of proving that a contract is not to be regarded as a consumer contract shall lie on the seller'; and

(ii) the definition of 'quality' is omitted;

(b) subsection (2) is omitted; and

(c) after subsection (5) there is inserted—

'(5A) References in this Act to dealing as consumer are to be construed in accordance with Part I of the Unfair Contract Terms Act 1977; and, for the purposes of this Act, it is for a seller claiming that the buyer does not deal as consumer to show that he does not.'

(10) For the heading 'Conditions and warranties' that precedes sections 10 to 14 there is substituted the heading 'Implied terms etc.'.

The Supply of Goods and Services Act 1982 (c. 29)

6.—(1) The Supply of Goods and Services Act 1982 is amended as follows.

(2) In section 1 (the contracts concerned), in subsections (1) and (3) after 'Act' there is inserted 'in its application to England and Wales and Northern Ireland'.

(3) In section 4 (contracts for transfer: quality or fitness) for subsections (2) and (3) there is substituted—

'(2) Where, under such a contract, the transferor transfers the property in goods in the course of a business, there is an implied condition that the goods supplied under the contract are of satisfactory quality.

(2A) For the purposes of this section and section 5 below, goods are of satisfactory quality if they meet the standard that a reasonable person would

APPENDIX III

regard as satisfactory, taking account of any description of the goods, the price (if relevant) and all the other relevant circumstances.

(3) The condition implied by subsection (2) above does not extend to any matter making the quality of goods unsatisfactory—

(a) which is specifically drawn to the transferee's attention before the contract is made,

(b) where the transferee examines the goods before the contract is made, which that examination ought to reveal, or

(c) where the property in the goods is transferred by reference to a sample, which would have been apparent on a reasonable examination of the sample.';

and subsection (9) is omitted.

(4) In section 5 (transfer by sample)—

(a) in subsection (2)(c), for 'rendering them unmerchantable' there is substituted 'making their quality unsatisfactory'; and

(b) subsection (3) is omitted.

(5) After section 5 there is inserted the following section—

'5A. Modification of remedies for breach of statutory condition in non-consumer cases

5A.—(1) Where in the case of a contract for the transfer of goods—

(a) the transferee would, apart from this subsection, have the right to treat the contract as repudiated by reason of a breach on the part of the transferor of a term implied by section 3, 4 or 5(2)(a) or (c) above, but

(b) the breach is so slight that it would be unreasonable for him to do so,

then, if the transferee does not deal as consumer, the breach is not to be treated as a breach of condition but may be treated as a breach of warranty.

(2) This section applies unless a contrary intention appears in, or is to be implied from, the contract.

(3) It is for the transferor to show that a breach fell within subsection (1)(b) above.'

(6) In section 6 (the contracts concerned) in subsections (1) and (3) after 'Act' there is inserted 'in its application to England and Wales and Northern Ireland'.

(7) In section 9 (contracts for hire: quality or fitness) for subsections (2) and (3) there is substituted—

'(2) Where, under such a contract, the bailor bails goods in the course of a business, there is an implied condition that the goods supplied under the contract are of satisfactory quality.

(2A) For the purposes of this section and section 10 below, goods are of satisfactory quality if they meet the standard that a reasonable person would regard as satisfactory, taking account of any description of the goods, the consideration for the bailment (if relevant) and all the other relevant circumstances.

(3) The condition implied by subsection (2) above does not extend to any matter making the quality of goods unsatisfactory—

(a) which is specifically drawn to the bailee's attention before the contract is made,

(b) where the bailee examines the goods before the contract is made, which that examination ought to reveal, or

(c) where the goods are bailed by reference to a sample, which would have been apparent on a reasonable examination of the sample.';

and subsection (9) is omitted.

(8) In section 10 (hire by sample)—

(a) in subsection (2)(c), for 'rendering them unmerchantable' there is substituted 'making their quality unsatisfactory'; and

(b) subsection (3) is omitted.

(9) After section 10 there is inserted the following section—

'**10A. Modification of remedies for breach of statutory condition in non-consumer cases**
(1) Where in the case of a contract for the hire of goods—

(a) the bailee would, apart from this subsection, have the right to treat the contract as repudiated by reason of a breach on the part of the bailor of a term implied by section 8, 9 or 10(2)(a) or (c) above, but

(b) the breach is so slight that it would be unreasonable for him to do so,

then, if the bailee does not deal as consumer, the breach is not to be treated as a breach of condition but may be treated as a breach of warranty.

APPENDIX III

(2) This section applies unless a contrary intention appears in, or is to be implied from, the contract.

(3) It is for the bailor to show that a breach fell within subsection (1)(b) above.'

(10) In section 18 (interpretation) in subsection (1) the definition of 'quality' is omitted and at the end of that section there is inserted—

'(3) For the purposes of this Act, the quality of goods includes their state and condition and the following (among others) are in appropriate cases aspects of the quality of goods—

(a) fitness for all the purposes for which goods of the kind in question are commonly supplied,

(b) appearance and finish,

(c) freedom from minor defects,

(d) safety, and

(e) durability.

(4) References in this Act to dealing as consumer are to be construed in accordance with Part I of the Unfair Contract Terms Act 1977; and, for the purposes of this Act, it is for the transferor or bailor claiming that the transferee or bailee does not deal as consumer to show that he does not.'

SALE AND SUPPLY OF GOODS

SCHEDULE 3 REPEALS

Section 7

Chapter	Short title	Extent of repeal
1973 c. 13.	The Supply of Goods (Implied Terms) Act 1973.	In section 15, in subsection (1), the words from '"condition" and "warranty"' to 'material to the agreement' and subsection (2).
1979 c. 54.	The Sale of Goods Act 1979.	Section 11(5). Section 15(2)(b). Section 30(4). In section 34, the words from the beginning to '(2)'. In section 61, in subsection (1) the definition of 'quality' and subsection (2).
1982 c. 29.	The Supply of Goods and Services Act 1982.	Section 4(9). Section 5(3). Section ((9). Section 10(3). Section 17(1). In section 18(1), the definition of "quality" and in the definition of 'goods' the words '), other than things in action and money'.

Appendix IV

Legislative provisions amended by the Sale and Supply of Goods Act 1994

Amended Legislative Provisions: Sale of Goods Act 1979, sections 14, 15, 15A, 30, 34, 35 & 35A

14. Implied terms about quality or fitness

(1) Except as provided by this section and section 15 below and subject to any other enactment, there is no implied term about the quality or fitness for any particular purpose of goods supplied under a contract of sale.

(2) Where the seller sells goods in the course of a business, there is an implied term that the goods supplied under the contract are of satisfactory quality.

(2A) For the purposes of this Act, goods are of satisfactory quality if they meet the standard that a reasonable person would regard as satisfactory, taking account of any description of the goods, the price (if relevant) and all the other relevant circumstances.

(2B) For the purposes of this Act, the quality of goods includes their state and condition and the following (among others) are in appropriate cases aspects of the quality of goods:-

(a) fitness for all the purposes for which goods of the kind in question are commonly supplied;

(b) appearance and finish;

(c) freedom from minor defects;

(d) safety; and

(e) durability.

(2C) The term implied by subsection (2) above does not extend to any matter making the quality of goods unsatisfactory:-

(a) which is specifically drawn to the buyer's attention before the contract is made,

(b) where the buyer examines the goods before the contract is made, which that examination ought to reveal, or

(c) in the case of a contract for sale by sample, which would have been apparent on a reasonable examination of the sample.

(3) Where the seller sells goods in the course of a business and the buyer, expressly or by implication, makes known:-

(a) to the seller, or

(b) where the purchase price or part of it is payable by instalments and the goods were previously sold by a credit-broker to the seller, to that credit-broker,

any particular purpose for which the goods are being bought, there is an implied term that the goods supplied under the contract are reasonably fit for that purpose, whether or not that is a purpose for which such goods are commonly supplied, except where the circumstances show that the buyer does not rely, or that it is unreasonable for him to rely, on the skill or judgement of the seller or credit-broker.

(4) An implied term about quality or fitness for a particular purpose may be annexed to a contract of sale by usage.

(5) The preceding provisions of this section apply to a sale by a person who in the course of a business is acting as agent for another as they apply to a sale by a principal in the course of a business, except where that other is not selling in the course of a business and either the buyer knows that fact or reasonable steps are taken to bring it to the notice of the buyer before the contract is made.

(6) As regards England and Wales and Northern Ireland the terms implied by subsections (2) and (3) above are conditions.

(7) Paragraph 5 of Schedule 1 below applies in relation to a contract made on or after 18 May 1973 and before the appointed day,* and paragraph 6 in relation to one made before 18 May 1973.

(8) In subsection (7) above and paragraph 5 of Schedule 1 below references to the appointed day are to the day appointed for the purposes of those provisions by an order of the Secretary of State made by statutory instrument.

*19 May 1985 (SI 1983/1572)

APPENDIX IV

15. Sale by sample

(1) A contract of sale is a contract for sale by sample where there is an express or implied term to that effect in the contract.

(2) In the case of a contract for sale by sample there is an implied condition:-

   (a) that the bulk will correspond with the sample in quality;

   [(b) repealed]

   (c) that the goods will be free from any defect, making their quality unsatisfactory, which would not be apparent on reasonable examination of the sample.

(3) As regards England and Wales and Northern Ireland, the term implied by subsection (2) above is a condition.

(4) Paragraph 7 of Schedule 1 below applies in relation to a contract made before 18 May 1973.

15A. Modifications of remedies for breach of condition in non-consumer cases

(1) Where in the case of a contract of sale:-

   (a) the buyer would apart from this subsection, have the right to reject goods by reason of a breach on the part of the seller of a term implied by section 13, 14 or 15 above, but

   (b) the breach is so slight that it would be unreasonable for him to reject them,

   then, if the buyer does not deal as consumer, the breach is not to be treated as a breach of condition but may be treated as a breach of warranty.

(2) This section applies unless a contrary intention appears in, or is to be implied from, the contract.

(3) It is for the seller to show that a breach fell within subsection (1)(b) above.

(4) This section does not apply to Scotland.

34. Buyer's right of examining the goods

Unless otherwise agreed, when the seller tenders delivery of goods to the buyer, he is bound on request to afford the buyer a reasonable opportunity of examining the goods for the purpose of ascertaining whether they are in conformity with the contract and, in the case of a contract for sale by sample, of comparing the bulk with the sample.

SALE AND SUPPLY OF GOODS

35. Acceptance

(1) The buyer is deemed to have accepted the goods subject to subsection (2) below:-

   (a) when he intimates to the seller that he has accepted them, or

   (b) when the goods have been delivered to him and he does any act in relation to them which is inconsistent with the ownership of the seller.

(2) Where goods are delivered to the buyer, and he has not previously examined them, he is deemed to have accepted them under subsection (1) above until he has had a reasonable opportunity of examining them for the purpose:-

   (a) of ascertaining whether they are in conformity with the contract, and

   (b) in the case of a contract for sale by sample, of comparing the bulk with the sample.

(3) Where the buyer deals as consumer or (in Scotland) the contract of sale is a consumer contract, the buyer cannot lose his right to rely on subsection (2) above by agreement, waiver or otherwise.

(4) The buyer is also deemed to have accepted the goods when after the lapse of a reasonable time he retains the goods without intimating to the seller that he has rejected them.

(5) The questions that are material in determining for the purposes of subsection (4) above whether a reasonable time has elapsed include whether the buyer has had a reasonable opportunity of examining the goods for the purpose mentioned in subsection (2) above.

(6) The buyer is not by virtue of this section deemed to have accepted the goods merely because:-

   (a) he asks for, or agrees to, their repair by or under an arrangement with the seller, or

   (b) the goods are delivered to another under a sub-sale or other disposition.

(7) Where the contract is for the sale of goods making one or more commercial units, a buyer accepting any goods included in a unit is deemed to have accepted all the goods making the unit; and in this subsection 'commercial unit' means a unit division of which would materially impair the value of the goods or the character of the unit.

(8) Paragraph 10 of Schedule 1 below applies in relation to a contract made before 22 April 1967 or (in the application of this Act to Northern Ireland) 28 July 1967.

APPENDIX IV

35A. Right of partial rejection

(1) If the buyer

    (a) has the right to reject the goods by reason of a breach on the part of the seller that affects some or all of them, but

    (b) accepts some of the goods, including, where there are any goods unaffected by the breach, all such goods,

he does not by accepting them lose his right to reject the rest.

(2) In the case of a buyer having the right to reject an instalment of goods, subsection (1) above applies as if references to the goods, were reference to the goods comprised in the instalment.

(3) For the purposes of subsection (1) above, goods are affected by a breach if by reason of the breach they are not in conformity with the contract.

(4) This section applies unless a contrary intention appears in, or is to be implied from, the contract.

(To avoid too much repetition the amended provisions in the context of other contracts for the supply of goods have not been included.)

Appendix V

Specimen Contract for Sale

_____ LIMITED
CONDITIONS OF SALE

1. Parties
The parties to this contract are _____ Limited ("the seller") and the customer named overleaf ("the buyer"). This contract is not assignable by the buyer without the written consent of the seller.

2. Contract exclusively subject to these conditions
(a) These conditions supersede any other conditions previously issued.

(b) This contract contains the entire bargain between the seller and the buyer and, in the case of any inconsistency between these terms and the terms of any other contract document sent by the buyer to the seller (whatever their respective dates) in respect of the goods, these terms shall prevail.

(c) Buyer's Standard Conditions of Purchase shall not apply unless specifically accepted in advance and in writing by a director of the seller.

3. Variation of terms
These conditions may not be varied except by the written consent of a director of the seller.

4. The price
(a) The price of the goods ("the price") shall be that specified in the contract.

(b) Where applicable Value Added Tax will be applied in accordance with United Kingdom legislation at the tax point date.

(c) The seller reserves the right by notice given at any time before delivery to vary the price if, after the date of the contract, there is an increase in the total cost of the goods to the seller owing to wars, Queen's enemies, defence measures, imposition of new customs, excise, or other duties or taxes, increase in the costs of raw materials or labour, scarcity of labour or any other cause whatsoever.

SALE AND SUPPLY OF GOODS

(d) If any variation to the price under condition 4(c) shall increase the price by more than 10 per cent over the price ruling at the date of the contract, the buyer may cancel the contract or any undelivered balance of the contract by written notice to the seller, served within three days of receipt of the seller's notice under condition 4(c).

(e) In the event that the buyer fails to take delivery of any part of the goods, the seller shall be entitled, by giving notice to the buyer in writing, to increase the price of the goods remaining undelivered to the seller's standard price or the price ruling on the actual date of delivery.

5. Payment

(a) Invoices dated 20th–19th of any month are due for payment by the 10th of the subsequent month.

(b) Payments made within 7 days of the invoice date are allowed a settlement discount of 3¾ per cent.

(c) Payments made by the 10th of the following month as per (a) above are allowed a settlement discount of 2½ per cent.

(d) Payments made within 30 days of the invoice date will be net and no discount will be allowed on them.

(e) If any payment is not made on or before the due date, the seller reserves the right to charge interest at 3 per cent per annum above the base lending rate of Barclays Bank PLC. Such interest shall run from day to day and shall accrue after as well as before any judgment and shall be compounded monthly on the amounts overdue until payment thereof.

6. Delivery of goods

(a) Delivery date(s) means the date(s) upon which the goods are ready for despatch to the point of delivery specified by the buyer.

(b) Unless otherwise agreed in writing, any period for delivery shall be calculated from the date of the seller's receipt of the order. The seller will make every effort to observe delivery requirements but any stipulated dates or requirements for delivery are estimates only.

(c) The seller shall not be liable for any loss or damage whether arising directly or indirectly from delay in delivery.

(d) Each delivery of a quantity of goods under this contract shall be deemed to constitute a separate contract to which the terms and conditions hereof apply.

APPENDIX V

(e) The seller will endeavour to deliver the correct quantities of goods ordered, but this is dependent on stocks being available and the seller shall not be liable for short delivery, and the buyer shall only be obliged to pay for the actual quantities of goods delivered.

(f) Should expedited delivery be agreed and necessitate overtime or additional costs, such costs and overtime expenses are to be borne by the buyer.

7. Risk
The risk in the goods shall pass to the buyer upon delivery of the goods to the buyer.

8. Carriage of goods
Carriage will be chargeable on all sales under £100.

9. Damage or loss in transit
The seller will repair or replace, free of charge, goods lost or damaged in transit where delivery has been made by the seller's carrier, provided that the buyer shall give to the seller written notification of such loss or damage within 10 days of receipt of the seller's invoice.

10. Warranties
(a) The goods are warranted to comply with the specification set out in the order of if there is no such specification to be of normal commercial quality or the quality which is otherwise customary for the type of goods concerned.

(b) Where the buyer has specified that the goods are to be of a certain colour, finish, size or design, such specification shall be subject to reasonable commercial variation.

(c) The seller shall not be liable for breach of any of the terms implied by the Sale of Goods Act 1979 relating to description, quality, fitness for purpose, or for any defects in the goods arising from faulty materials or manufacture unless the buyer notifies the seller in writing within 14 days of receipt of the goods of such defects. The seller shall not be liable in respect of any goods which have been processed, cut or altered in any way, or not used in a proper manner.

11. Claims for loss or damage
(a) The seller shall not be liable for any loss of or damage to the goods or loss of or damage to commercial or industrial property caused by the goods, however caused or arising, unless the buyer notifies the seller in writing, in the case of loss of or damage to the goods within 14 days of receipt of the goods, and in the case of loss

SALE AND SUPPLY OF GOODS

of or damage to commercial property within 14 days of the occurrence of such loss or damage.

(b) The seller shall not be liable for any indirect or consequential loss however caused.

Appendix VI

Specimen Contract for the Hire of Goods

TERMS AND CONDITIONS

1. Parties
This contract is made between the Leasing Company Limited (hereinafter called "the company") and the hirer.

2. Exclusivity of terms
This agreement supersedes any previous terms and conditions.

3. The subject-matter of the contract
The company agrees to let the equipment described overleaf to the hirer.

4. The duration of the agreement
The company agrees to let the equipment to the hirer for the term stated overleaf. The term shall commence on the arrival of the equipment at the location specified overleaf.

5. Amount of the rental
[This will no doubt be stated on the face of the rental form.]

6. Payment of the rental
(a) Subject to (b) and (c) below, the rental shall be due and payable in full, together with VAT, within seven days of the arrival of the equipment at the specified location, and it shall be the aggregate of the instalments shown overleaf.

(b) Provided that the hirer fulfils all obligations as set out in this agreement, he may pay the rental by the instalments plus VAT as set out overleaf. The first instalment shall be due and payable at the commencement of the term.

(c) Should the hirer fail to pay any such instalment on its due date, the company shall be entitled to immediate payment of the outstanding balance of the rental upon demand.

SALE AND SUPPLY OF GOODS

7. Ownership of the goods
The equipment shall remain the company's exclusive property and the hirer shall not commit or permit any act which conflicts with the company's right of ownership.

8. Obligations of the hirer
(a) The hirer shall not cause or permit the equipment to be removed from the premises indicated overleaf without the prior written consent of the company.

(b) The hirer shall maintain the equipment in good working order and repair, ensure that it is kept safe and without risk to health, and observe all the manufacturer's and/or supplier's instructions relating to its use and operation.

9. Risk
The hirer shall assume the entire risk of damage to or loss of the equipment or any part thereof and shall forthwith upon arrival effect and shall maintain until termination of this agreement comprehensive insurance in respect of the equipment for its full replacement value.

10. Quality and fitness of the goods
Except as provided in this agreement, or except where the hirer is a consumer, all warranties and conditions arising out of statutes are hereby expressly excluded.

11. Defective goods
If the equipment should prove in any way defective the hirer shall give the company written notice within seven days of discovering the defect.

12. Loss or damage
The hirer hereby indemnifies the company against all claims, demands and costs howsoever caused, arising out of any loss or damage caused by the use of the equipment.

13. Manufacturers' guarantees
The company shall transfer or assign to the hirer the benefit of any warranty or guarantee relating to the equipment granted to the company by any supplier or manufacturer thereof.

14. Cancellation of the contract
Should the hirer commit any breach of this agreement, the company shall be entitled forthwith to terminate this agreement by giving written notice to the hirer and/or by retaking possession of the equipment.

15. Notices
Any notice to be given under this contract to the company or the hirer may be deemed delivered if despatched to the addresses shown overleaf.

16. The making of claims
The company will not entertain any claims by the hirer unless such claims are made in writing in accordance with the terms of this agreement.

Appendix VII

Specimen Hire-Purchase Agreement

TERMS OF THE AGREEMENT

1. Payment
Before signing this agreement you must have paid the deposit shown overleaf. By signing this agreement you agree to pay the Balance Payable by making the payments set out overleaf, by their specified dates, to us at the address given overleaf or to any person or address notified by us in writing. Punctual payment is essential. If you pay by post you do so at your own risk.

2. Failure to pay on time
We have the right to charge interest at the annual percentage rate shown overleaf on all overdue amounts. This interest will be calculated on a daily basis from the date the amount falls due until it is received and will run both before and after any judgment.

3. Ownership of the goods
You will become the owner of the goods only after we have received all amounts payable under this agreement including under Clauses 2 and 11. Until then the goods remain our property and your rights are solely those of a hirer.

4. Selling or disposing of the goods
You must keep the goods safely at your address and you may not sell or dispose of them or transfer your rights under this agreement. You may only part with the goods to have them repaired. You may not use the goods as security for any of you obligations.

5. Repair of the goods
You must keep the goods in good condition and repair at your own expense. You are responsible for all loss of or damage to them (except fair wear and tear) even if caused by acts or events outside your control. You must now allow a repairer or any other person to obtain a lien on or a right to retain the goods.

SALE AND SUPPLY OF GOODS

6. Change of address
You must immediately notify us in writing of any change of your address.

7. Inspection
You must allow us or our representative to inspect and test the goods at all reasonable times.

8 Insurance
You must keep the goods insured under a fully comprehensive policy of insurance at your own expense. You must notify us of loss of or damage to the goods and hold any monies payable under the policy in trust for us. You irrevocably authorise us to collect the monies from the insurers. If a claim is made against the insurers we may at our absolute discretion conduct any negotiations and effect any settlement with the insurers and you agree to abide by such settlement.

9. Your right to end the agreement
You have the right to end this agreement as set out in the notice 'Termination: Your Rights' overleaf. You must then at your own expense return the goods to us.

10. Our right to end the agreement
We may end this agreement, after giving you written notice, if:

(a) you fail to keep to any of the terms of this agreement;

(b) you commit any act of bankruptcy or have a receiving, interim or bankruptcy order made against you or you petition for your own bankruptcy, or are served with a creditor's demand under the Insolvency Act 1986 or the Bankruptcy (Scotland) Act 1985, or make a formal composition or scheme with your creditors, or call a meeting of them;

(c) you make a formal composition with or call a meeting of your creditors;

(d) execution is levied or attempted against any of your assets or income or, in Scotland, your possessions are pounded or your wages arrested;

(e) the landlord of the premises where the goods are kept threatens or takes any step to distrain on the goods or, in Scotland, exercises his right of hypothec over them;

(f) where you are a partnership, the partnership is dissolved;

(g) you have given false information in connection with your entry into this agreement;

(h) the goods are destroyed or the insurers treat a claim under the above policy on a total loss basis.

APPENDIX VII

If we end this agreement then, subject to your rights as set out in the notice 'Repossession: Your Rights' overleaf, we may retake the goods. You will also then have to pay to us all overdue payments, and such further amount as is required to make up one half of the Total Amount Payable under this agreement. If you have failed to take reasonable care of the goods you may have to compensate us for this.

11. Expenses
You must repay on demand our expenses and legal costs for:

(a) finding your address if you change address without immediately informing us or finding the goods if they are not at the address given by you;

(b) taking steps, including court action, to recover the goods or to obtain payment for them.

12. Exclusion
(a) If you are dealing as consumer (as defined in the Unfair Contract Terms Act 1977) nothing in this agreement will affect your rights under the Supply of Goods (Implied Terms) Act 1983.

(b) In all other cases:

   (i) you rely on your own skill and judgement as to the quality of the goods and their fitness for their intended purpose;

   (ii) we will not b responsible for their quality, their fitness for any purpose or their correspondence with any description or specification.

13. General provisions
(a) The word 'goods' includes replacements, renewals and additions which we or you may make to them with our consent.

(b) No relaxation or indulgence which we may extend to you shall affect our strict rights under this agreement.

(c) Where two or more persons are named as the customer, you jointly and severally accept the obligations under this agreement. This means that each of you can be held fully responsible under this agreement.

(d) We may transfer our rights under this agreement.

14. When this agreement takes effect
This agreement will only take effect if and when it is signed by us or our authorised representative.

SALE AND SUPPLY OF GOODS

IMPORTANT – YOU SHOULD READ THIS CAREFULLY
YOUR RIGHTS

The Consumer Credit Act 1974 covers this agreement and lays down certain requirements for your protection which must be satisfied when the agreement is made. If they are not, we cannot enforce the agreement against you without a court order.

The Act also gives you a number of rights. You have a right to settle this agreement at any time by giving notice in writing and paying off all amounts payable under the agreement which may be reduced by a rebate.

If you would like to know more about the protection and remedies provided under the Act, you should contact either your local Trading Standards Department or your nearest Citizens' Advice Bureau.

Index

Acceptance, 2, 54, 84
  examination, and, 38, 56
  inconsistent act, by, 38
  intimation, by, 38
  lapse of reasonable time, by, 39
  loss of right to reject by, 36-8
  partial, 3
Actio quanti minoris, 44
Affirmation, (*see also* **Acceptance**), 36
Agent
  liability of, 28
  obligations owed by, 28
  private seller, acting through, 27-9
  quality obligation, 30
  sale by, 27, 28

Breach of contract, (*see also* **Remedies** and **Acceptance**), 33-46, 65
  loss of right to reject by acceptance, 36
  reasonableness and right to reject, 35
  remedies, summary of, 45
  right to reject, 34
  Scottish law, 34, 60, 61, 74
  slight or immaterial breaches, 34, 35
Burden of proof on supplier, 12
Business seller, 21
  family member, sale to, 22
  friend, sale to, 22

Commercial sales
  exempt liability for, 11, 30
Commercial buyer
  right to reject, 3
Common law, 1, 36

Consequential loss
  exclusion of, 15
Consumer
  dealing as, 10, 49
  definition of, 10
Contracts
  not made in the course of a business, 10
Contract term
  limitation clauses, and, 11
  requirement of reasonableness, 11
  variation, 87
  warranties, 89
Criminal liability, 21, 22

Damages, 43, 45, 60, 61
  breach of quality obligation, 2
  description, for, 43
  disappointment, for, 45
  exemption clauses, and, 45
  fitness for purpose, for, 43
  injury, for, 45
  loss of profits, 44, 45
  property, damage to, 45
  quality, for, 43
  reduction in value, for, 45
Dangerous undertaking, 15
Dealing as a consumer, *see* **Consumer**
Defects
  examination for, 26
  goods, right to reject, 43
  latent, 40
  minor, freedom from, 30
  non-functional, 25

SALE AND SUPPLY OF GOODS

Defects — *cont.*
  partial rejection, and, 41
  seller's duty to point out, 26-7
  specifically pointed out, 26
Delivery
  wrong quantity, 53
Description, 30
  quality standard, and, 23-4
Durability, 30
  old definition of, 26
  requirement for, 26
Duty of care, 16
  exclusion for breach, 9, 13

Examination, *see* **Goods**
Excluding liability, 8-9, 11, 15, 29
  commercial sales, in, 11, 27
  difficulty of task, and, 15
  implied terms, 29
  right to reject, for, 40
Exemption clauses, 3, 7-17, 45, 49
  agents, in connection with, 29
  commercial sales, in, 11, 30
  damages, and, 45
  definition under UCTA, 8
  durability, and, 26
  excluding liability, 8
  fitness for purposes, use of, 24
  insurance, and, 15, 16, 25, 40
  Law Commission report, 28
  limitation of liability, and, 11
  negligence, and, 15
  quality obligation, and, 9, 27
  reasonableness test, 11-17
  restricting liability, 8
  summary of, 27
  trade bodies, and, 25
  transparency of, 40

Fitness for purposes, 30
  exemption clauses, use of, 24
  limitations on, 24

Fitness for purposes — *cont.*
  sellers, implications for, 24
  uncommon purpose, buyer with, 25

Goods
  damage to, 89
  delivery, 88
  durability, requirement for, 26
  defects, *see* **Defects**
  examination of, 26, 54, 56, 83
  fitness for purposes, 24
  payment, 88
  private use or consumption, for, 10
  repair, 41
  replacement, 41
  right to reject, *see* **Right to reject**
  second hand, 26
  transfer, *see* **Transfer of Goods**

Hire contracts
  SSGA Schedules, and, 21
  terms and conditions, 91
Hire purchase contracts
  SSGA Schedules, and, 21
  terms, 95

Immaterial breaches
  contracting out of rules on, 35-6
Implied terms, 1
  damages for breach, 43
  description, 9, 11, 63, 66
  exclusion of, 29, 68
  extension of, 1
  fitness, 9, 11, 52, 53, 63, 67
  quality, 9, 11, 52, 53, 55, 63, 67
  restriction of, 29
  right to reject, and, 34
  samples, 64, 68, 83
  title, 62
  transfer of possession, 66

INDEX

Insurance, 40
  buyers, and, 15, 16, 25
  suppliers, and, 15

Latent defect, 40
Law Commission, 22, 28
Liability, 29
  criminal, 21, 22
  exclusion of, 8-9, 11
  private seller, 27
  restriction of, 8-9, 11, 29
  sub-buyers, to, 45
Limitation clauses, 12, 15, 29
Limitations on purposes
  drawing attention to, 24
Losses
  calculation of, 43
  exclusion of, 14
  mitigate, requirement to, 45
  remoteness, 45
  setting off against price, 44

Merchantable quality, *see* **Merchantability standard**
Merchantability standard, 5
  replacement by quality standard, 20, 24, 25
Minor defects
  freedom from, 30

Negligence
  agent, liability for, 28
  exemption clauses, and, 15
  seller, action of, 29
Non-functional defects, 25
  exempting liability for, 26

Partial rejection
  right of, 41, 57, 85
Payment, 88
Price
  reduction of, 23, 45

Price — *cont.*
  setting off losses against, 44
  quality standard, effect on, 23
Private buyer, 10, 11
Private seller, 29
  business agent, acting through, 27-9

Quality obligation (*see also* **Quality standard**), 2, 3, 19-31
  breaches of, 28
  checklist for application, 30
  damages for breach, 2
  exemption, and, 8-17
  key cases, 31
  not applicable, when, 30
  section 14(1) SGA, 20
  selling in course of a business, 21-3
Quality standard, (*see also* **Quality obligation**), 23-31
  agent, and, 27
  buyer with uncommon purpose, and, 25
  durability, 26
  defects and examination, 26-7
  description, importance of, 23-4
  exemption, and, 8-17, 24-5, 27
  exempting liability for non-functional defects, and, 26
  fitness for purposes, 24
  liability of private seller acting through business agent, 27-9
  limitations on purposes, 24
  merchantability standard, replacement of, 20, 24
  minor defect, and, 23
  non-functional problems, and, 24-5
  price, effect on, 23
  sale by agent in course of business, and, 27
  second hand goods, for, 26
  test for, 23
  unsafe goods, and, 23

SALE AND SUPPLY OF GOODS

Reasonableness test, 11-17, 48, 50
  alternatives, 14
  bargaining power, and, 13-14
  burden of proof, 12
  consequences of, 16
  contract term, for, 11
  difficulty of task, and, 15-16
  immaterial breaches, 34
  insurance, and, 16
  key decisions, and, 13
  limitation clauses, and, 11
  practical consequences of, 16
  right to reject, and, 35
  schedule 2 criteria, 11-12
  slight breaches, 34
Reject, *see* **Right to reject**
Remedies, breach of contract for, 3, 25, 33-46, 59, 65
  damages, *see* **Damages**
  exemption clauses, and, 40
  key cases, 46
  losses, setting off against price, 33
  right to reject, *see* **Right to reject**
  slight or immaterial breaches, 34, 35
  summary of, 45
  termination, buyer's choice to, 41
Repair, 39, 41
Replacement, 41
Reporting defects, 15
Restricting liability, 8-9
Right to reject, (*see also* **Remedies and Acceptance**), 3, 34, 57
  buyer's choice as to termination, 41-4
  commercial buyer, 3
  defective goods, 43
  exclusion of, 40
  exemption clauses, and, 40, 45
  implied terms, and, 34
  introduction, 34
  limitation of, 40
  loss by acceptance, 2, 3, 36-9

Right to reject — *cont.*
  partial rejection, 3, 41, 57, 85
  reasonableness, and, 35
  slight or immaterial breaches, for, 3, 34

Safety, 9, 30
Sale and Supply of Goods Act 1994
  reforms made by, 5
Sample
  sale by, 53, 64, 68, 83
Satisfactory quality standard, *see* **Quality standard**
Scotland, 1, 2, 3, 8, 10, 11, 28, 34, 35, 36, 40, 43, 44, 60, 61, 74
  reasonable time rule, 40
  slight breach, 34, 35, 36
Second hand goods
  quality standard for, 26
Selling in course of business, (*see also* **Business seller**), 21-2
Setting off losses against price, 44
  actio quanti minoris, 44
Slight breaches
  contracting out of rules on, 35-6

Term, *see* **Contract term**, **Implied terms**
Termination,
  buyer's choice as to, 41-4
Transfer of goods, contracts for, 27, 29, 64, 66
  SSGA Schedules, and, 21
  UCTA controls, 29

Uncommon purpose
  buyer with, 25
Undisclosed principal, 28

Warranty
  condition, treated as, 51
Withholding price, 44